Long-Term Care Policies and Procedures

A Self-Care Approach

Laura Ann Luc, RN, MSN

Gerontological Clinical Nurse Specialist

Rush-Presbyterian-St. Luke's Medical Center

Chicago, Illinois

Michele Beattie, RN, BSN

Geriatric Assessment/Admission Coordinator

Rush-Presbyterian-St. Luke's Medical Center

Chicago, Illinois

AN ASPEN PUBLICATION®

Aspen Publishers, Inc.

Gaithersburg, Maryland

1993

Library of Congress Cataloging-in-Publication Data

Luc, Laura Ann.
Long-term care policies and procedures : a self-care approach /
Laura Ann Luc, Michele Beattie.
p.   cm.
Includes bibliographical references and index.
ISBN 0-8342-0320-0
1. Geriatric nursing—Handbooks, manuals, etc. I. Beattie,
Michele. II. Title.
[DNLM: 1. Geriatric Nursing—methods—outlines. 2. Long-Term
Care—in old age—nurses' instruction. 3. Long-Term Care—in old
age—outlines. 4. Nursing Process—outlines. WY
18 L931L]
RC954.L8 1993
610.73'65—dc20
DNLM/DLC
for Library of Congress
92-48193
CIP

Illustrations copyright © 1992 by
Carol Luc

The authors have made every effort to ensure the accuracy of the information herein. However, appropriate
information sources should be consulted, especially for new or unfamiliar procedures. It is the responsibility of every practitioner to evaluate the appropriateness of a particular opinion in the context of actual clinical situations and with due consideration to new developments. Authors, editors, and the publisher cannot
be held responsible for any typographical or other errors found in this book.

Editorial Resources: Barbara Priest

Library of Congress Catalog Card Number: 92-48193
ISBN: 0-8342-0320-0

Printed in the United States of America

1 2 3 4 5

For Rich Jeffries

From you I learned the value of caring for self, supporting
others, and striving for wholeness. You are in my heart.

L.A.L.

* * * *

For all of the older adults who have allowed me the
privilege of knowing them, learning from them, and
assisting them through their difficult times. Thank you
for helping me to understand.

* * * *

To my grandmother, an extraordinary woman who passed
away as this volume was being concluded. I'll miss you.

M.B.

Table of Contents

Contributor

Carol Luc, M.A.

Illustrator
Detroit, Michigan

Preface

Prior to utilizing this text, it is imperative to understand three concepts used throughout. The first two concepts have been chosen to reinforce gerontologic thinking. The third concept describes the relationship between procedure objectives and evaluations.

First, specific pronouns have been carefully chosen for use within this text. They reflect current trends in population statistics and gerontologic awareness. The United States Census Bureau projects that the number of Americans aged 65 and over will double between 1980 and 2020. Persons aged 65 and over made up 12 percent of the population in 1982, or 25 million people, and are expected to make up 17 percent of the population by 2020.

Older women outnumber older men three to two, compared with a ratio of five to four in 1960. This disparity further increases among those aged 85 and over (American Nurses' Association, 1987, p. 21). Since there is a greater number of older women in the population, the pronoun she/he is used in the text to reflect this statistic. It should also bring to the readers' consciousness the fact that they will be in contact with a large group of older women in both their professional nursing practice and personal life.

Second, the use of the term *resident* expresses an awareness of the relationship between the older person and her/his environment. Resident refers to the fact that a person lives or resides at a specific location. For example, a resident of an apartment complex, a resident of a nursing home, a resident of a city. The use of the word *client* denotes a temporary relationship, one in which there is a service that is contracted for and provided to that person. *Resident* is used throughout this text to reinforce the concepts of independence and autonomy that should be respected and promoted for individuals in their own environment.

Lastly, there are defined objectives and evaluations for each procedure. Objectives describe the goals of the procedures. Evaluation describes those procedure outcomes that let us know whether or not the objectives have been met. Evaluation includes the resident's physical response to a procedure as well as the resident's expressed feelings about the situation.

REFERENCE

American Nurses' Association. (1987). *Standards and scope of gerontological nursing practice.* Kansas City, MO: Author.

chapter 1

Framework

Wellness is a concept of maximal importance to gerontology and gerontological nursing and is the driving force behind our actions as practitioners. Wellness encompasses the highest level of health, well-being, and quality of life possible for an older individual. Whether we practice in long-term care, community, or acute care settings, we aspire to a certain level of wellness for our clients.

An older person's level of wellness is reflected in her/his ability to maintain maximum overall functioning even with the occurrence of physical changes related to aging and perhaps the presence of one or more chronic illnesses. Functioning is defined as a person's ability to complete ADL (activities of daily living) and IADL (instrumental activities of daily living). ADL and IADL are basic activities that one needs to perform in order to care for oneself and one's surroundings. ADL include bathing, dressing, grooming, toileting, ambulating, and eating. IADL include medication administration, shopping, meal preparation, housework, money management, telephone use, laundry, and transportation. The nurse's role in interacting with older people is to foster achievement and maintenance of an individual's own level of wellness. This principle can be demonstrated in all phases of the nursing process: assessment, concern identification, intervention, and evaluation, and subsequently in all of our client interactions.

NURSING THEORY

One important way to incorporate the idea of wellness in our own individual nursing practice is to base our practice on a nursing theory. Nursing theory "will give the professional nurse a strong base of knowledge on which to practice and explain[s] the approach to nursing care" (George, 1990, p. 12). It is an organized way of connecting what we do with why we do it. There are many different nursing theories that provide unique ways to address the core concepts of nursing, health, person, and environment. The nursing theory we choose as individual professionals influences us during all levels of the nursing process and becomes the internal philosophy that governs our practice.

Dorothea Orem's general theory of nursing looks at self care and the nurse's role within self care and is tangential to the ideas of wellness and functioning. It is composed of three separate but related theories:

1. self-care theory
2. self-care deficit theory
3. the theory of nursing systems

In the self-care theory, Orem defines self care as the "practice of activities that individuals initiate and perform on their own behalf in maintaining life, health and well-being" (George, 1990, p. 92). Self-care agency is the human ability to perform self care. The actions of self care are directed toward certain requirements. Orem labels these requirements as three categories of self-care requisites: universal, developmental, and health deviation. "Universal self-care requisites are common to all human beings and include the maintenance of air, water, food, elimination, activity and rest, and solitude and social interaction, prevention of hazards and promotion of human functioning" (Marriner-Tomey, 1989, p. 120). Developmental self-care requisites are those requirements related to a certain developmental stage or a circumstance related to that stage, for example, adjusting to retirement or relocation. Health deviation self-care requisites are those requirements that are a result of disease, injury, or a change in health state. The therapeutic self-care demand is composed of all self-care actions needed to address and meet the self-care requisites.

The self-care deficit theory describes when nursing is needed. Nursing is needed when the therapeutic self-care demand is greater than an individual's self-care ability. The person cannot do all that is necessary to fulfill the universal, developmental, and/or health deviation requirements.

The theory of nursing systems describes three different ways that nurses are involved in addressing a client's self-care requisites.

1. In the *wholly compensatory* nursing system the nurse compensates for the client's inability to perform self care by actually doing the care for the client.
2. In the *partly compensatory* nursing system both the nurse and client have active roles in completion of self-care requirements.
3. The *supportive-educative* nursing system provides education by the nurse to the client while the client performs self care.

Orem states that a client can utilize one or more of these systems.

Example of Theory Utilization

The following demonstrates the use of Orem's general theory in conjunction with the nursing process in order to address a client's concerns.

Mrs. A. is an 82-year-old woman who relocated to an intermediate care facility (ICF) three weeks ago from her own home of 46 years.

Assessment

Subjective Data. (These data were obtained from Mrs. A. and her family.) Mrs. A. always had a good appetite. She ate three meals per day and occasionally snacked. She weighed 140 pounds last month at her physician's office. Mrs. A. has always made friends easily and was involved with her neighborhood. She states, "I just don't feel like eating. . .I prefer to be alone."

Objective Data. Mrs. A. weighs 135 pounds today. She ate half of her breakfast this morning and refused her lunch and dinner. Mrs. A. refuses to join in social activities. She relocated to the ICF from her home three weeks ago. Mrs. A. is physically able to open cartons and use utensils but does not do so at present.

Problem/Need (Self-Care Deficit). Alteration in nutrition related to relocation and depression. This self-care deficit is composed of demands in the universal self-care and developmental self-care areas. Mrs. A. cannot do all that is necessary to fulfill the universal and developmental requirements and so nursing is needed.

Plan

Partly Compensatory Nursing System. The nurse will assist the resident with tray, i.e., open cartons, etc., as needed. The nurse will verbally encourage the resident to be independent of food set up and will assist less often as the resident's independence increases.

Partly Compensatory Nursing System. The nurse and resident will maintain calorie count for four days. The resident will weigh self weekly.

Supportive-Educative Nursing System. The nurse will encourage the resident's verbalization of the relocation experience as needed. The nurse will acknowledge and support the resident's feelings regarding the change in environment.

Resident Goals

1. The resident will demonstrate increasing independence with food set up, i.e., opening cartons, preparing food by self, etc.
2. The resident will demonstrate an increasing amount of food intake daily until a total of 1,600 calories per day is maintained. Weight will steadily increase by one pound per week until ideal weight of 140 pounds is achieved.
3. The resident will begin to express feelings regarding relocation through verbalizations and sharing of emotions.

RATIONALE

It is important for the nurse to understand *why*, not just *how*, to apply basic nursing procedures when assisting residents to achieve their individual goals. For example, when an older person's level of wellness is reflected in her/his ability to maintain maximum overall functioning, then incorporation of Orem's general theory into gerontological nursing practice helps us to focus on wellness by identifying the client's self-care ability and acting to promote self care.

In the preceding example, the nurse utilizes the partly compensatory and supportive-educative nursing systems to promote and enhance the client's self care. Each client's goals reflect increasing independence and self care until the usual level of self care and functioning is achieved. Through utilization of Orem's general theory we can examine a client situation, identify client concerns, and base interventions and goals on principles of self care and autonomy. By impacting upon an older person's ability to complete her/his own ADL and IADL, we are fostering that person's perception and feeling of wellness.

The nurse can incorporate Orem's general theory, functional ability, and wellness in all areas of gerontological nursing practice. In gerontological nursing practice, "emphasis is placed on maximizing functional ability in the activities of daily living; promoting, maintaining, and restoring health, including mental health; preventing and minimizing the disabilities of acute and chronic illness; and maintaining life in dignity and comfort until death" (American Nurses' Association, 1987, p. 23). This emphasis can be seen in acute care, long-term care, and community care of older individuals.

In acute care, the life-threatening condition takes precedence. However, the concepts of self care and functioning can and should be addressed throughout hospitalization. Initially, the nurse obtains information regarding the client's functional ability prior to hospitalization from the client, family members, or other professionals involved in the client's daily life. This information aids in formulating realistic goals for the client. By incorporating current information about the client's health status with prehospitalization functional information and utilizing Orem's general theory, a step-by-step approach to increase and/or maintain health and independence can be developed and reflected in the care plan.

In both long-term care and community care, the goal of nursing is to "restore, maximize, and maintain a person's functional status and independence for as long as possible" (Becker & Cohen, 1984, p. 928). Again, utilization of Orem's general theory and concepts of functional ability and wellness provide a foundation to meet this goal.

When the concepts of self care form our internal, professional philosophy and can be reflected in utilization of the nursing process in all areas of gerontological nursing practice, then our view of policies and procedures and the nurse's and resident's role in them must also demonstrate a desire to promote self care. Traditionally, policies and procedures have been viewed as a doing to or doing for the resident. Incorporating self-care concepts within policies and procedures changes the focus from doing *for* to doing *with* and also encourages the resident to complete a task autonomously, if possible.

The following policies and procedures will utilize all three of Orem's nursing systems: the wholly compensatory nursing system, the partly compensatory nursing system, and the supportive-educative nursing system. The overall goal of these policies and procedures is to enhance and promote the resident's self care and autonomy. Depending upon the level of technical skill needed and the resident's ability to execute a task, varying amounts of nursing intervention are needed for procedure completion. Promotion of self care and autonomy in the context of policies and procedures can be demonstrated by encouraging residents to make choices regarding time and place for task completion and also by teaching the resident about a particular procedure. Policies and procedures reflecting principles of self care foster a communicative relationship between the nurse and resident while promoting feelings of wellness and independence in the resident.

In order to demonstrate the importance of functioning in daily interactions with residents, the ensuing policies and procedures have been organized according to ADL and IADL categories. The ADL section is composed of bathing and grooming, physical mobility, continence, and eating. The IADL section focuses exclusively on medications and bedmaking. The remaining section concentrates on health assessment/special skills. The nursing system(s) being utilized for each policy and procedure is designated in the upper right corner. This is a very practical demonstration of the relationship between self-care principles, functional ability, and daily nursing procedures.

ISSUES OF CONCERN

The premise of this text is that the promotion of self care is important in order to foster independence and functional ability in older people. Issues exist, however, that challenge us to examine our own perception of aging and self care. Our perception colors our ability to see growth and change in older people. Table 1-1 illustrates these issues and corresponding strategies that nurses can use to promote their own growth and change. Nurses' own growth and change ultimately influence their ability to promote the concept of self care during interactions with older adults.

Table 1-1 Growth Strategies

Issues	*Strategies*
Society devalues elderly people in our culture.	Contemplate our own aging. How do we want to feel? What do we want to be doing? How do we want others to respond to us?
	Observe ways that we convey ageist ideas in our own conversations and actions. How can we change this behavior and make others aware of the ageism in their own lives?
We maintain our identity and a sense of control in the world through the use of our bodies.	Think about ways that we identify ourselves through use of our bodies. How do we manage ourselves and the world around us?
	Consider how our perception of self might be altered if physical changes affected our ability to use our bodies and/or our ability to relate to others in our world.
The combination of the presence of chronic illness and disuse of our bodies can alter the performance of self care.	Think about the power we possess if we have a fit, well body. How does that impact upon our own self care? What might we feel like if our strength or health were compromised?
	Identify people experiencing chronic illness and disuse of their bodies and notice the impact, if any, on their ability to perform ADL and IADL.
Institutionalization decreases residents' autonomy.	Consider the amount of autonomy we currently possess in our everyday lives. How would a restricted environment affect the number of options available to us? How might we feel if we had limited options and freedom?

Table 1-2 General Teaching Strategies

Changes	Teaching Considerations
Hearing	
Loss of ability to hear high-pitched sounds; decreased ability to discriminate sounds; greater difficulty distinguishing words with *t, f, s, z, g.*	Speak in a regular voice; don't shout or raise your voice. Speak intentionally and distinctly. Sit close by and face the older person. Choose a quiet room without extraneous voices or distractions. If the older person wears a hearing aid, be sure it is in place and functioning.
Vision	
Diminished visual acuity with the field of vision not as sharp; lens becomes thicker and yellow, thereby distorting colors; increased difficulty with color discrimination; decreased amount of light reaches the retina due to a smaller pupil; decreased peripheral vision; changes in depth perception.	For visual aids, use large dark print on contrasting light background. Use soft light radiating from behind the older person and directed toward the visual aid. Allow time for older person to become familiar with any equipment used. If resident wears eyeglasses, be sure they are on and clean.
Memory and Cognitive Ability	
Decreased short-term memory; increased reaction time (it takes longer for an older person to respond); decreased ability to concentrate.	Give small amounts of pertinent information. Take time to teach psychomotor skills and encourage demonstration. Repeat information as necessary. Allow more time for the older person to respond.

TEACHING STRATEGIES

Throughout these policies and procedures there are many teaching opportunities. Whether a nurse is giving a resident information about a particular task or is teaching a resident to actually complete a task, the nurse is facilitating self care of the older individual through education. Education promotes increased independence in older people.

Older adults vary, reflecting their many years of growth and change. Experiences, educational level, and skills are just a few of the areas that impact upon the task of learning new ideas. Physical changes with age also influence one's ability to learn. Nurses need to consider all of these factors when preparing to teach an older individual. Appropriate teaching strategies are essential to foster learning and knowledge acquisition.

Table 1-2 illustrates general teaching strategies that address some common components of aging.

REFERENCES

American Nurses' Association. (1987). *Standards and scope of gerontological nursing practice.* Kansas City, MO: Author.

Becker, P., & Cohen, H. (1984). The functional approach to care of the elderly: A conceptual framework. *Journal of American Geriatrics Society, 32*(12), 923–929.

George, J. (Ed.). (1990). *Nursing theories: The base for professional nursing practice* (3rd ed.). Norwalk, CT: Appleton & Lange.

Marriner-Tomey, A. (1989). *Nursing theorists and their work* (2nd ed.). St. Louis: C.V. Mosby.

chapter 2

Bathing and Grooming

Nursing System

	Wholly Compensatory
✔	Partly Compensatory
✔	Supportive-Educative

BATH—BED

OBJECTIVES

1. To promote clean and intact skin
2. To maintain resident's overall hygiene and self esteem
3. To encourage resident's active involvement in completion of ADL

LEVEL OF RESPONSIBILITY

Registered nurse, licensed practical nurse, certified nursing assistant

POLICY

Each resident shall have two complete baths per week. Additional baths may be required to keep resident clean and odor free. Bed baths should only be done with those residents who are totally bed-bound and unable to be up in the chair.

EQUIPMENT

1. Basin and warm water
2. Towels, washcloth, soap, and body lotion

3. Clean clothing and other linen as needed
4. Manicure set
5. Orange stick

PROCEDURE	**RATIONALE**
1. *Encourage* resident to *choose* time for the bath.	The ability to choose promotes independence for the resident.
2. At agreed upon time, *explain* procedure to resident and bring equipment to bedside.	
3. Wash your hands.	Hand washing prevents the spread of infection.
4. Keep the room at a warm temperature.	This maintains the resident at a constant temperature and prevents chilling.
5. Offer bedpan to resident before starting the bath.	Voiding prior to bathing promotes the resident's comfort.
6. Loosen upper bedding. Cover resident with the sheet.	
7. Obtain warm bath water. Check temperature of water with your own hand and wrist.	
8. *Encourage* resident to do as much for self as possible. This could be any or all parts of the bathing activity, from applying soap on the washcloth to washing entire body parts. Use the following sequence for bathing:	Self performance of bathing and dressing activities promotes independence and encourages exercise and range of motion.
a. Wash face and ears. Rinse and dry carefully.	
b. Remove bedclothes, but keep resident covered with the sheet. Expose only those areas about to be washed.	
c. Wash neck, arms, chest, and abdomen.	
d. Wash thighs, legs, and feet.	
e. Change water.	
f. Wash back, buttocks, and genitalia.	
g. Discard bath water.	
9. *Encourage* resident to apply body lotion. *Assist* as necessary.	

PROCEDURE	RATIONALE
10. Replace resident's clothing. *Encourage* resident to select clothing to be worn. Also *encourage* resident to dress self as much as possible.	

11. Clean finger- and toenails. *Encourage* resident to perform activity as much as possible.
 	
   a. Remove any dirt or debris under nails with an orange stick.
 	
   b. Trim nails. Fingernails should be trimmed in a rounded fashion. Toenails should be trimmed straight across.
	Do not trim toenails of diabetic residents or residents with peripheral vascular disease. These residents should be referred to a podiatrist. A small cut in the skin could result in a subsequent infection.

12. Offer resident a brush and comb to groom her/his own hair.	This encourages independence and promotes shoulder and arm range of motion.
13. Remake the bed.	
14. Discard towels and used linen appropriately.	
15. Clean and remove equipment for storage or disposal.	
16. *Encourage* and *assist* resident as necessary to attain a comfortable position.	
17. Place call light within the resident's reach.	
18. Wash your hands.	Hand washing prevents the spread of infection.

DOCUMENTATION

1. Date and time of bath
2. Amount of self care that the resident was able to perform
3. Presence of any reddened or discolored skin areas, dry or irritated skin, or any other unusual findings
4. Signature and title of nursing staff member

EVALUATION

1. The resident's skin will be clean and intact.
2. The resident's overall hygiene and self esteem will be maintained.
3. The resident will be actively involved in completion of ADL.

Nursing System

	Wholly Compensatory
✔	Partly Compensatory
✔	Supportive-Educative

BATH—TUB

OBJECTIVES

1. To promote clean and intact skin
2. To maintain resident's overall hygiene and self esteem
3. To encourage resident's active involvement in completion of ADL

LEVEL OF RESPONSIBILITY

Registered nurse, licensed practical nurse, certified nursing assistant

POLICY

Each resident shall have two complete baths per week. Additional baths may be required to keep resident clean and odor free.

EQUIPMENT

1. Tub and warm water
2. Towels, washcloth, and body lotion
3. Bath mat
4. Clean clothing
5. Manicure set
6. Orange stick

PROCEDURE	RATIONALE
1. *Encourage* resident to *choose* time for the bath.	The ability to choose promotes independence for the resident.
2. At agreed upon time, *explain* procedure to resident and bring equipment to bathroom.	
3. Wash your hands.	Hand washing prevents the spread of infection.
4. Keep the room at a warm temperature.	This maintains the resident at a constant temperature and prevents chilling.
5. Place nonskid bath mat in tub. Obtain warm bath water. Check temperature of water with your own hand and wrist.	Use of nonskid mat provides a safe surface on which to stand.

PROCEDURE	RATIONALE
6. Offer resident opportunity to void prior to bathing.	Voiding prior to bathing promotes the resident's comfort.
7. *Encourage* resident to remove clothes. *Assist* as necessary.	
8. *Encourage* resident to get into tub with use of safety bar. *Assist* as necessary.	
9. *Encourage* resident to do as much for self as possible. This could be any or all parts of the bathing activity, from applying soap on the washcloth to washing entire body parts. Use the following sequence for bathing:	Self performance of bathing and dressing activities promotes independence and encourages exercise and range of motion.
a. Wash face and ears. Rinse and dry carefully.	
b. Wash neck, arms, chest, and abdomen.	
c. Wash back, buttocks, and genitalia.	
d. Wash thighs, legs, and feet.	
10. *Encourage* resident to get out of tub with use of safety bar. Offer resident a towel for drying self. *Encourage* application of lotion. *Assist* as necessary.	
11. Replace resident's clothing. *Encourage* resident to select clothing to be worn. Also *encourage* resident to dress self as much as possible.	
12. Clean finger- and toenails. *Encourage* resident to perform activity as much as possible.	Do not trim toenails of diabetic residents or residents with peripheral vascular disease. These residents should be referred to a podiatrist. A small cut in the skin could result in a subsequent infection.
a. Remove any dirt or debris under nails with an orange stick.	
b. Trim nails. Fingernails should be trimmed in a rounded fashion. Toenails should be trimmed straight across.	
13. Offer resident a brush and comb to groom her/his own hair.	This encourages independence and promotes shoulder and arm range of motion.
14. *Encourage* resident to decide his/her next activity. *Assist* resident to ambulate to next activity if necessary.	The ability to choose promotes independence for the resident.

PROCEDURE	RATIONALE
15. Discard towels and used linen appropriately.	
16. Clean and remove equipment for storage or disposal.	
17. Disinfect tub per infection control standards.	Tub disinfection promotes a clean environment and prevents the spread of infection.
18. Wash your hands.	Hand washing prevents the spread of infection.

DOCUMENTATION

1. Date and time of bath
2. Amount of self care that the resident was able to perform
3. Presence of any reddened or discolored skin areas, dry or irritated skin, or any other unusual findings
4. Signature and title of nursing staff member

EVALUATION

1. The resident's skin will be clean and intact.
2. The resident's overall hygiene and self esteem will be maintained.
3. The resident will be actively involved in completion of ADL.

Nursing System

Wholly Compensatory
✔ Partly Compensatory
✔ Supportive-Educative

DOUCHE (VAGINAL IRRIGATION)

OBJECTIVES

1. To cleanse vaginal tract of irritating or copious amounts of discharge
2. To soothe irritated vaginal area
3. To encourage resident's active involvement in completion of ADL

LEVEL OF RESPONSIBILITY

Registered nurse, licensed practical nurse

POLICY

Frequency of irrigation and type of solution will be ordered by physician. Universal precautions are used when nursing staff is assisting with this procedure.

EQUIPMENT

1. Vaginal irrigation set
2. Solution as ordered by physician
3. Nonsterile gloves
4. Protective pad
5. Bedpan
6. Gown and eye protectors
7. Dressings or perineal pads as needed
8. Bath blanket

PROCEDURE	RATIONALE
1. *Encourage* resident to *choose* the time for vaginal irrigation.	The ability to choose promotes independence for the resident.
2. At agreed upon time, *explain* the procedure and purpose to the resident.	
3. Prepare solution as ordered by the physician using clean technique. Temperature of	This provides a comfortable temperature for the client.

PROCEDURE	RATIONALE
solution should be warm (105 degrees Fahrenheit or 40.5 degrees Celsius).	
4. *Encourage* resident to go to the bathroom for the procedure if possible. Resident may sit on toilet for this activity.	
5. If resident is unable to ambulate to the bathroom, *assist* to a lithotomy position (see Appendix B) on the bedpan with a protective pad under buttocks and bedpan. Drape with bath blanket. Hips should be higher than shoulders.	This allows solution to flow into vagina.
6. Assemble equipment needed and screen for privacy.	
7. *Encourage* resident to void.	Insertion of vaginal nozzle will be easier if bladder is empty. Also, there will be less likelihood for cramping if bladder is empty.
8. *Encourage* resident to do as much of the vaginal irrigation procedure as possible.	Self performance of activities of daily living promotes independence and encourages exercise and range of motion.
9. Put on gloves, gown, and eye protectors if assisting with any portion of the procedure.	Use of gloves protects both the resident and the nurse and prevents the spread of infection. Use of a gown and eye protectors is required to comply with universal precautions.
10. Position irrigation bag containing prepared solution on IV pole, or hang from hook or towel bar approximately 12 inches above vaginal opening.	
11. Lubricate nozzle and insert approximately 2 inches into the vagina. Direction will be upward and backward to follow the curvature of the vagina.	
12. Irrigation should be at a slow rate. Rotate nozzle gently while inserting into the vagina. Use all of the prescribed solution.	This facilitates insertion without causing irritation.
13. When all of the prescribed solution has been used, withdraw the tip of the catheter gently. Inspect tissues of labia for irritation or excoriation. Inspect contents of bedpan or toilet.	
14. *Encourage* resident to dry perineum with clean towel.	

PROCEDURE	RATIONALE
15. If resident requires perineal pads or dressings, *offer assistance* to resident, or apply at this time.	
16. *Encourage* resident to ask questions regarding the procedure. *Offer encouragement* for resident's participation in self care.	
17. Remove gloves, gown, and eye protectors. Dispose of properly.	
18. Dispose of all equipment properly.	
19. Wash your hands.	Hand washing prevents the spread of infection.
20. *Assist* resident to a comfortable position with call light within reach if resident is bedbound.	

DOCUMENTATION

1. Date and time of treatment
2. Amount and temperature of solution used, type of solution including any medications added, strength, and amounts
3. Characteristics of return flow, noting whether return was cloudy or clear, any changes in color, odors that may be present
4. Condition of the perineum, noting redness, excoriation, edema, tenderness
5. Signature and title of nursing staff member

EVALUATION

1. Resident will understand the need for the vaginal irrigation.
2. Resident will tolerate the procedure well and participate in the self-care process.
3. There will be no irritation of vaginal or perineal tissues.

Nursing System

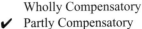

	Wholly Compensatory
✔	Partly Compensatory
✔	Supportive-Educative

FINGERNAIL CARE

OBJECTIVES

1. To promote clean nails
2. To maintain resident's overall hygiene and self esteem
3. To encourage resident's active involvement in completion of ADL

LEVEL OF RESPONSIBILITY

Registered nurse, licensed practical nurse, certified nursing assistant

POLICY

Each resident shall have her/his fingernails cared for at least twice per week during bath times. Additional nail care may be necessary to maintain hygiene.

EQUIPMENT

1. Basin and warm water
2. Manicure set
3. Towel
4. Orange stick
5. Hand lotion

PROCEDURE	RATIONALE
1. *Encourage* resident to *choose* time for nail care.	The ability to choose promotes independence for the resident.
2. At agreed time, *explain* procedure to resident and assemble equipment.	
3. Wash your hands.	Hand washing prevents the spread of infection.
4. *Encourage* resident to do as much for self as possible. This could be any or all parts of the nail care activity. Use the following sequence for nail care:	Self performance of nail care activity promotes independence and encourages range of motion.

PROCEDURE	RATIONALE
a. Arrange towel underneath resident's hands.	
b. Soak hands in basin half full of warm water for 10 to 20 minutes.	Soaking softens nails and removes dirt and debris.
c. Remove hands from basin and place on towel.	
d. Remove any dirt or debris under nails with an orange stick.	
e. Trim nails. Fingernails should be trimmed in a rounded fashion.	Trimming fingernails in a rounded fashion prevents accidental scratches or injury to self from pointed nail ends.
f. Apply and massage lotion onto hands.	
5. Discard towel appropriately.	
6. Clean and remove equipment for storage or disposal.	
7. Wash your hands.	Hand washing prevents the spread of infection.

DOCUMENTATION

1. Date and time of nail care
2. Amount of self care that the resident was able to perform
3. Presence of any dryness, open areas, or drainage
4. Signature and title of nursing staff member

EVALUATION

1. The resident's nails will be clean.
2. The resident's overall hygiene and self esteem will be maintained.
3. The resident will be actively involved in completion of ADL.

	Wholly Compensatory
✔	Partly Compensatory
✔	Supportive-Educative

FOOT CARE

OBJECTIVES

1. To promote and maintain skin integrity of the feet
2. To encourage the resident's active involvement in completion of ADL

LEVEL OF RESPONSIBILITY

Registered nurse, licensed practical nurse, certified nursing assistant

POLICY

Each resident's feet will be soaked and inspected daily.

EQUIPMENT

1. Large basin
2. Soap solution
3. Bath towels
4. Washcloth
5. Pitcher of clean warm water
6. Manicure set
7. Orange stick

PROCEDURE	RATIONALE
1. *Encourage* resident to *choose* the time for foot care.	The ability to choose promotes independence for the resident.
2. At agreed upon time, *explain* procedure to resident and gather equipment.	
3. Wash your hands.	Hand washing prevents the spread of infection.
4. *Encourage* resident to do as much for self as possible. This could be any or all parts of foot care, from assembling equipment to completion of foot care process. Use the following sequence for foot care:	Self performance of activities of daily living promotes independence and encourages exercise and range of motion.

PROCEDURE	RATIONALE
a. Fill basin with lukewarm water and mild soap solution. Check water temperature with your wrist.	Residents with vascular disease may not be able to feel hot temperatures on their feet. Subsequently, they may experience a burn if the water is too warm.
b. Soak feet 10 to 15 minutes.	
c. Rinse thoroughly with clean lukewarm water.	
d. Blot feet dry with a soft towel. Dry carefully between toes.	Prolonged moisture, especially between toes, promotes fungus growth.
e. If feet are rough and dry, rub them with moisture-restoring cream or lotion recommended by a podiatrist.	
f. Remove any dirt or debris remaining under nails with an orange stick.	
g. Trim toenails straight across, even with the ends of the toes.	Do not trim toenails of diabetic residents or residents with peripheral vascular disease. These residents should be referred to a podiatrist. A small cut in the skin could result in a subsequent infection.
h. Use clean absorbent stockings and supportive nonskid shoes.	Clean absorbent stockings promote intact skin. Supportive shoes promote safe mobility.
5. Discard towels appropriately.	
6. Clean and remove equipment for storage or disposal.	
7. Wash your hands.	Hand washing prevents the spread of infection.

DOCUMENTATION

1. Date and time of foot care
2. Amount of self care that the resident was able to perform
3. Presence of any reddened or discolored skin areas, swelling, cracks in the skin, sores, or dryness
4. Referral to a podiatrist, if necessary
5. Signature and title of nursing staff member

EVALUATION

1. Skin integrity of the resident's feet will be maintained.
2. The resident will be actively involved in completion of ADL.

Nursing System

Wholly Compensatory ✔ Partly Compensatory ✔ Supportive-Educative

HAIR AND SCALP CARE

OBJECTIVES

1. To promote clean and healthy hair
2. To maintain resident's overall hygiene and self esteem
3. To encourage resident's active involvement in completion of ADL

LEVEL OF RESPONSIBILITY

Registered nurse, licensed practical nurse, certified nursing assistant

POLICY

Each resident shall have her/his hair combed at least daily. Each resident shall have a shampoo weekly.

EQUIPMENT

1. Comb and brush
2. Shampoo
3. Conditioner
4. Towels

PROCEDURE	RATIONALE
1. *Encourage* resident to *choose* time for hair care.	The ability to choose promotes independence for the resident.
2. At agreed upon time, *explain* procedure to resident and assemble equipment.	
3. Wash your hands.	Hand washing prevents the spread of infection.
4. *Encourage* resident to brush and comb hair to remove all tangles. *Assist* as necessary.	
5. If a shampoo is to be completed, use the following sequence. For residents who have difficulty standing for longer periods of time, the shampoo may take place in the shower or at a salon-style sink, if available.	The action of a forward head tilt demands strength, flexibility, and balance skills.

PROCEDURE	RATIONALE
For residents with greater strength, flexibility, and balance, the resident may wash hair at the bathroom sink. *Encourage* resident to do as much for self as possible. This could be any or all parts of the shampoo activity.	Self performance of shampoo activities promotes independence and encourages exercise and range of motion.
a. Wet hair with water.	
b. Apply shampoo to hair. Massage hair and scalp well.	
c. Rinse until all shampoo is removed.	
d. Apply tangle free conditioner to hair.	
e. Rinse until all conditioner is removed.	
f. Towel dry hair.	
g. Comb hair to remove any tangles and promote drying.	
6. *Encourage* resident to style own hair. Ascertain resident's style preference and *assist* if necessary.	
7. Discard towels appropriately.	
8. Clean and remove equipment for storage or disposal.	
9. Wash your hands.	Hand washing prevents the spread of infection.

DOCUMENTATION

1. Date and time of shampoo
2. Amount of self care that the resident was able to perform
3. Presence of the following:

    a. Patches of hair loss
    b. Pediculosis: especially tiny nits on hair stems, behind ears, on crown of head, and on occiput
    c. Localized areas of redness and tenderness
    d. Sores or scratches
    e. Pigmentations, ulcerations, or raised growths

4. Signature and title of nursing staff member

EVALUATION

1. The resident's hair will be clean and healthy.
2. The resident's overall hygiene and self esteem will be maintained.
3. The resident will be actively involved in completion of ADL.

Nursing System

✔ Wholly Compensatory
✔ Partly Compensatory
✔ Supportive-Educative

NIGHTTIME CARE

OBJECTIVES

1. To maintain resident's overall hygiene and self esteem
2. To encourage restful sleep
3. To encourage the resident's active involvement in completion of ADL

LEVEL OF RESPONSIBILITY

Registered nurse, licensed practical nurse, certified nursing assistant

POLICY

Each resident will have access to nighttime care every night. Nighttime care consists of a combination of activities and procedures to ready a resident for sleep. The nighttime care procedure refers to the equipment lists and steps for those procedures that constitute nighttime care.

EQUIPMENT

Refer to equipment lists for:

1. Oral hygiene
2. Perineal care
3. Back rub

PROCEDURE	RATIONALE
1. *Encourage* resident to *choose* time for nighttime care.	The ability to choose promotes independence for the resident and also assists the resident to maintain her/his lifelong, sleep/awake patterns.
2. At agreed upon time, *explain* procedure to resident and assemble equipment.	
3. Wash your hands.	Hand washing prevents the spread of infection.
4. *Encourage* resident to do as much for self as possible. This could be any or all of the nighttime care activity. Use the following sequence for nighttime care:	Self performance of nighttime care activities promotes independence and encourages exercise and range of motion.

PROCEDURE	RATIONALE
a. *Encourage* resident to ambulate to bathroom to void. *Encourage* use of bedpan if bedbound.	
b. *Encourage* resident to complete oral care and perineal care. Refer to these individual procedures.	
c. Offer the resident an opportunity for a back rub. Refer to back rub procedure.	
5. As the nursing staff member, complete the following steps:	
a. Provide adequate blankets for warmth.	
b. Provide fresh water within easy reach of the resident.	
c. Check resident's call lights and response system.	
6. Wash your hands.	Hand washing prevents the spread of infection.

DOCUMENTATION

1. Date and time of nighttime care
2. Amount of self care that the resident was able to perform
3. Documentation as per oral hygiene, perineal care, and back rub procedures
4. Signature and title of nursing staff member

EVALUATION

1. The resident's overall hygiene and self esteem will be maintained.
2. The resident will experience restful sleep.
3. The resident will be actively involved in completion of ADL.

Nursing System

	Wholly Compensatory
✔	Partly Compensatory
✔	Supportive-Educative

ORAL HYGIENE

OBJECTIVES

1. To maintain resident's overall hygiene and self esteem
2. To promote clean teeth and mouth, which will enhance appetite
3. To encourage resident's active involvement in completion of ADL

LEVEL OF RESPONSIBILITY

Registered nurse, licensed practical nurse, certified nursing assistant

POLICY

Oral hygiene shall be provided to residents at least three times daily: in the morning upon rising, after lunch, and at night.

EQUIPMENT

1. Toothbrush
2. Toothpaste
3. Mouthwash and water
4. Cup and straw
5. Emesis basin or access to sink
6. Face towel
7. Denture cup
8. Nonsterile gloves

PROCEDURE	RATIONALE
1. *Encourage* resident to *choose* time for oral care.	The ability to choose promotes independence for the resident.
2. At agreed upon time, *explain* procedure to resident and assemble equipment.	
3. Wash your hands.	Hand washing prevents the spread of infection.
4. *Encourage* resident to attain a standing or sitting position. If ambulatory, standing or sitting in front of the bathroom sink is ideal. Otherwise, *encourage* resident to sit	Facilitating a familiar posture for an activity encourages independence in that activity.

PROCEDURE	RATIONALE
up in chair or sit up in bed. *Assist* resident with transfer or ambulation if necessary.	
5. Continue with appropriate steps for tooth brushing and or denture care.	

Tooth Brushing

PROCEDURE	RATIONALE
1. Keep equipment within easy reach of the resident. *Encourage* resident to do as much for self as possible. This could be any or all parts of oral care. Use the following sequence for tooth brushing:	Self performance of oral care activities promotes independence and encourages exercise and range of motion.
a. Put small amount of toothpaste on toothbrush.	
b. Brush teeth downward on the upper teeth and upward on the lower teeth from the gum line to the crown.	
c. Rinse mouth frequently using solution of one half water and one half mouthwash.	
d. Dry face with a towel.	
2. Discard towels appropriately.	
3. Clean and remove equipment for storage or disposal.	
4. Wash your hands.	Hand washing prevents the spread of infection.

Denture Care

PROCEDURE	RATIONALE
1. Keep equipment within easy reach of the resident. *Encourage* resident to do as much for self as possible. This could be any or all parts of oral care. If nursing staff member performs oral care activity, put on nonsterile gloves. Use the following sequence for denture care:	Self performance of oral care activities promotes independence and encourages exercise and range of motion.
	Gloves are to be worn when touching mucous membranes. This prevents the spread of infection and follows universal precautions.
a. Remove dentures and place in denture cup.	
b. Put small amount of toothpaste on toothbrush and brush dentures under running cool water.	

PROCEDURE	RATIONALE
c. Inspect dentures for rough areas or breaks.	Dentures are very fragile and need to be inspected regularly for cracks or rough areas.
d. Place dentures in cup with solution of mouthwash. Keep dentures in denture container until ready for use.	To maintain integrity and increase longevity of dentures, they need to be stored in a moist environment, i.e., clean mouthwash solution.
e. Clean natural teeth as per tooth brushing instructions.	
f. Dry face with a towel.	
2. Discard towel appropriately.	
3. Clean and remove equipment for storage or disposal.	
4. Wash your hands.	Hand washing prevents the spread of infection.

DOCUMENTATION

1. Date and time of oral care
2. Amount of self care that the resident was able to perform
3. Presence of any red, swollen, or tender areas of mouth, gums, or lips, or any oral bleeding
4. Condition of teeth and/or dentures
5. Signature and title of nursing staff member

EVALUATION

1. The resident's overall hygiene and self esteem will be maintained.
2. The resident's teeth and mouth will be clean.
3. The resident will be actively involved in completion of ADL.

> ✔   Wholly Compensatory
> ✔   Partly Compensatory
> ✔   Supportive-Educative

PERINEAL CARE

OBJECTIVES

1. To keep perineum clean, dry, and odor free
2. To promote skin integrity of the perineal area
3. To maintain resident's overall hygiene and self esteem
4. To encourage resident's active involvement in completion of ADL

LEVEL OF RESPONSIBILITY

Registered nurse, licensed practical nurse, certified nursing assistant

POLICY

Perineal care shall be completed each day during the morning bath. Additional perineal care may be necessary to keep resident clean and odor free.

EQUIPMENT

1. Basin with soap and water
2. Bedpan, if necessary
3. Disposable wipes
4. Pericare bottle, if necessary
5. Nonsterile gloves

PROCEDURE	RATIONALE
1. *Encourage* resident to *choose* time for perineal care.	The ability to choose promotes independence for the resident.
2. At agreed upon time, *explain* procedure to resident and assemble equipment.	
3. Wash your hands.	Hand washing prevents the spread of infection.
4. *Encourage* resident to do as much for self as possible. This could be any or all parts of perineal care activity. Use the appropriate steps for either ambulatory or bedbound resident.	Self performance of perineal care activity promotes independence and encourages exercise and range of motion.

PROCEDURE	**RATIONALE**

Perineal Care for Ambulatory Resident

1. *Encourage* resident to ambulate to bathroom. *Assist* if necessary.

2. Expose perineal area.

3. *Encourage* resident to perform self care of the activity. If nursing staff member assists with perineal care, wear nonsterile gloves.

   Gloves are to be worn when touching mucous membranes. This prevents the spread of infection and follows universal precautions.

4. Wash perineal area with soap and water. Use disposable wipes and cleanse from pubis to perineum. Use one stroke per wipe and then discard.

   Cleansing from pubis to perineum prevents fecal contamination of urethral and vaginal areas.

5. Rinse perineal area with clean warm water and wipes. Rinse from pubis to perineum.

6. Dry perineal area with clean disposable wipes from pubis to perineum.

7. Clean and remove equipment for storage or disposal.

8. Wash your hands.

   Hand washing prevents the spread of infection.

Perineal Care for Bedbound Resident

1. If nursing staff member performs perineal care activity, put on nonsterile gloves.

   Gloves are to be worn when touching mucous membranes. This prevents the spread of infection and follows universal precautions.

2. *Encourage* resident to sit on bedpan.

3. Expose perineal area.

4. Wash perineal area with soap and water. Use disposable wipes and cleanse from pubis to perineum. Use one stroke per wipe and then discard.

   Cleansing from pubis to perineum prevents fecal contamination of urethral and vaginal areas.

5. Using pericare bottle, pour clean warm water over perineal area to rinse.

6. Remove bedpan.

7. Dry perineal area with clean disposable wipes from pubis to perineum.

PROCEDURE	RATIONALE
8. Clean and remove equipment for storage or disposal.	
9. Wash your hands.	

DOCUMENTATION

1. Date and time of perineal care
2. Amount of self care that the resident was able to perform
3. Presence of any reddened or discolored skin areas, dry or irritated skin, or any other unusual findings
4. Presence of odor or discharge, color, amount, and location of discharge if present
5. Signature and title of nursing staff member

EVALUATION

1. The resident's perineum will be clean, dry, and odor free.
2. The skin of the perineal area will be intact and without irritation.
3. The resident's overall hygiene and self esteem will be maintained.
4. The resident will be actively involved in completion of ADL.

Nursing System

Wholly Compensatory
✔ Partly Compensatory
✔ Supportive-Educative

SHAVING MALE RESIDENTS

OBJECTIVES

1. To promote cleanliness and care of facial hair
2. To maintain resident's overall hygiene and self esteem
3. To encourage the resident's active involvement in completion of ADL

LEVEL OF RESPONSIBILITY

Registered nurse, licensed practical nurse, certified nursing assistant

POLICY

Male residents will have a shave at least two times per week and more often if facial hair growth is heavy.

EQUIPMENT

1. The individual resident's own nonelectric razor or disposable razor
2. Basin or sink
3. Bath towels
4. Washcloth
5. Shaving cream
6. After-shave lotion
7. Mirror
8. Chair, if needed

PROCEDURE	RATIONALE
1. *Encourage* resident to *choose* time for shave.	The ability to choose promotes independence for the resident.
2. At agreed upon time, *explain* procedure to resident and assemble equipment.	
3. Wash your hands.	Hand washing prevents the spread of infection.
4. *Encourage* resident to ambulate to sink. If able to, resident can stand at sink to perform self care. If not able to stand for a long period of time, resident can sit in chair facing sink with a mirror easily accessible.	Familiar locations and positions for self-care activities promote self care.

PROCEDURE	RATIONALE
5. Encourage resident to do as much for self as possible. This could be any or all parts of the shaving activity. Use the following sequence for shaving:	Self performance of shaving activity promotes independence and encourages exercise and range of motion.
a. Fill basin or sink half full of hot water.	
b. Apply moderately hot washcloth to face.	The application of a hot washcloth and then shaving cream softens the beard and aids in shaving.
c. Apply shaving cream.	
d. Pull skin tight in opposite direction to razor and shave beard.	
e. Rinse razor frequently.	
f. When completed, rinse face with warm water. Dry face and apply after-shave lotion.	
6. Clean and remove equipment for storage or disposal.	
7. Wash your hands.	Hand washing prevents the spread of infection.

DOCUMENTATION

1. Date and time of shave
2. Amount of self care that the resident was able to perform
3. Presence of any dry skin, skin lesions, or any discolorations
4. Signature and title of nursing staff member

EVALUATION

1. The resident's facial hair will be clean and cared for.
2. The resident's overall hygiene and self esteem will be maintained.
3. The resident will be actively involved in completion of ADL.

Nursing System

	Wholly Compensatory
✔	Partly Compensatory
✔	Supportive-Educative

SHOWER

OBJECTIVES

1. To promote clean and intact skin
2. To maintain resident's overall hygiene and self esteem
3. To encourage resident's active involvement in completion of ADL

LEVEL OF RESPONSIBILITY

Registered nurse, licensed practical nurse, certified nursing assistant

POLICY

Each resident shall have two complete showers/baths per week. Additional baths may be required to keep resident clean and odor free.

EQUIPMENT

1. Shower room and warm water
2. Towels, washcloth, soap, and body lotion
3. Shower chair, if necessary
4. Clean clothing
5. Manicure set
6. Orange stick

PROCEDURE	RATIONALE
1. *Encourage* resident to *choose* time for the bath.	The ability to choose promotes independence for the resident.
2. At agreed upon time, *explain* procedure to resident and bring equipment to bathroom.	
3. Wash your hands.	Hand washing prevents the spread of infection.
4. Keep the room at a warm temperature.	This maintains the resident at a constant temperature and prevents chilling.
5. Arrange shower chair in shower room, if resident needs use of chair.	Use of shower chair promotes resident's stability during shower. Chair should be used with those residents who experience fatigue or unsteadiness with standing for a short time.

PROCEDURE	RATIONALE
6. Offer resident opportunity to void prior to showering.	Voiding prior to showering promotes the resident's comfort.
7. Turn on shower and set warm water. Check temperature of water with your own hand and wrist.	
8. *Encourage* resident to remove clothes. *Assist* as necessary.	
9. *Encourage* resident to get under shower or to sit on shower chair. *Assist* as necessary.	
10. *Encourage* resident to do as much for self as possible. This could be any or all parts of the showering activity from applying soap on the washcloth to washing entire body parts. Use the following sequence for showering: a. Wash face and ears. Rinse carefully. b. Wash neck, arms, chest, and abdomen. c. Wash back, buttocks, and genitalia. d. Wash thighs, legs, and feet.	Self performance of bathing and dressing activities promotes independence and encourages exercise and range of motion.
11. *Encourage* resident to rinse self thoroughly, dry thoroughly, and apply body lotion. *Assist* as necessary.	
12. *Encourage* resident to get out of shower or up from shower chair. *Assist* as necessary.	
13. *Encourage* resident to select clothing to be worn. Also *encourage* resident to dress self as much as possible.	
14. Clean finger- and toenails. *Encourage* resident to perform activity as much as possible. a. Remove any dirt or debris under nails with an orange stick. b. Trim nails. Fingernails should be trimmed in a rounded fashion. Toenails should be trimmed straight across.	Do not trim toenails of diabetic residents or residents with peripheral vascular disease. These residents should be referred to a podiatrist. A small cut in the skin could result in a subsequent infection.
15. Offer resident a brush and comb to groom her/his own hair.	This encourages independence and promotes shoulder and arm range of motion.

PROCEDURE	**RATIONALE**
16. *Encourage* resident to *choose* her/his next activity. If necessary, *assist* resident to ambulate there.	The ability to choose promotes independence for the resident.
17. Discard towels and used linen appropriately.	
18. Clean and remove equipment for storage or disposal.	
19. Disinfect shower per infection control standards.	Shower disinfection promotes a clean environment and prevents the spread of infection.
20. Wash your hands.	Hand washing prevents the spread of infection.

DOCUMENTATION

1. Date and time of shower
2. Amount of self care that the resident was able to perform
3. Presence of any reddened or discolored skin areas, dry or irritated skin, or any other unusual findings
4. Signature and title of nursing staff member

EVALUATION

1. The resident's skin will be clean and intact.
2. The resident's overall hygiene and self esteem will be maintained.
3. The resident will be actively involved in completion of ADL.

chapter 3

Physical Mobility

Nursing System

	Wholly Compensatory
✔	Partly Compensatory
✔	Supportive-Educative

AMBULATION

OBJECTIVES

1. To increase the resident's level of flexibility, strength, and endurance
2. To increase circulation and minimize the risk of developing skin breakdown
3. To encourage the resident's active involvement in completion of ADL

LEVEL OF RESPONSIBILITY

Registered nurse, licensed practical nurse, certified nursing assistant

POLICY

Each resident who is able to walk will be encouraged to walk and, if necessary, assisted with ambulation at least three times per day.

EQUIPMENT

1. Supportive, comfortable walking shoes for the resident
2. Gait belt (if necessary)

PROCEDURE	**RATIONALE**
1. *Encourage* resident to *choose* time for ambulation.	The ability to choose promotes independence for the resident.
2. At agreed upon time, *explain* procedure to resident. Focus on ambulation goals for the present ambulation session.	Focusing on goals fosters a sense of progress, achievement, and future for the resident.
3. Wash your hands.	Hand washing prevents the spread of infection.
4. *Encourage* and/or *assist* resident to assume a sitting position and to put on nonskid, supportive footwear.	Proper footwear enhances ambulation ability.
5. Depending on the resident's ability, she/he may need assistance in one or more of the following steps:	
a. *Encourage* resident to assume an upright, standing position. Feet should be planted on the floor, head should be raised and looking forward.	An upright position promotes good balance and is imperative to successful ambulation.
b. *Encourage* resident to support self by holding onto your arm and/or by using guard rails in the hallway. Use gait belt as necessary.	
c. *Give* resident *encouragement*. Praise efforts and successes.	Acknowledgment of efforts and successes increases the resident's self esteem.
d. Observe the resident's endurance. If resident becomes weak or very tired, stay with the resident and call for assistance. Use a wheelchair to return resident to a chair or bed.	Continual observation of the resident prevents overexertion.
6. At completion of ambulation, *encourage* resident to *choose* location to rest, e.g., room, lounge, etc.	The ability to choose promotes independence for the resident.
7. Wash your hands.	Hand washing prevents the spread of infection.

DOCUMENTATION

1. Date and time of ambulation
2. Distance resident ambulated and her/his level of endurance
3. Amount of support/assistance the resident required
4. If ambulation is abruptly stopped due to the resident's intolerance, document the circumstance, a description of the resident (appearance, vital signs), and all nursing action taken
5. Signature and title of nursing staff member

EVALUATION

1. The resident's level of flexibility, strength, and endurance will be gradually increased.
2. The resident will be without areas of skin breakdown.
3. The resident will be actively involved in completion of ADL.

Nursing System

	Wholly Compensatory
✔	Partly Compensatory
✔	Supportive-Educative

AMBULATION WITH CANE

OBJECTIVES

1. To promote the resident's safety and stability during ambulation
2. To increase the resident's level of flexibility, balance, strength, and endurance
3. To increase circulation and minimize the risk of developing skin breakdown
4. To encourage the resident's active involvement in completion of ADL

LEVEL OF RESPONSIBILITY

Registered nurse, licensed practical nurse, certified nursing assistant

POLICY

Each resident who is able to walk will be encouraged to walk and, if necessary, assisted with ambulation at least three times per day.

EQUIPMENT

1. Cane (Figure 3-1)
2. Supportive, comfortable walking shoes for the resident

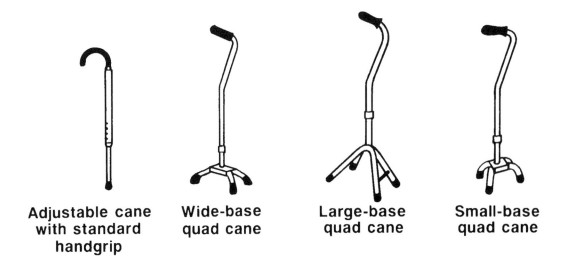

Adjustable cane with standard handgrip   Wide-base quad cane   Large-base quad cane   Small-base quad cane

Figure 3-1 Types of Walking Canes.

PROCEDURE	RATIONALE
1. *Encourage* resident to *choose* time for ambulation.	The ability to choose promotes independence for the resident.
2. At agreed upon time, *explain* procedure to resident. Focus on ambulation goals for the present ambulation session.	Focusing on goals fosters a sense of progress, achievement, and future for the resident.
3. Wash your hands.	Hand washing prevents the spread of infection.
4. *Encourage* and/or *assist* resident to assume a sitting position and to put on nonskid, supportive footwear.	Proper footwear enhances ambulation ability.
5. Depending on the resident's ability, she/he may need assistance in one or more of the following steps:	
a. *Encourage* resident to assume an upright, standing position. Feet should be planted on the floor, head should be raised and looking forward.	An upright position promotes good balance and is imperative to successful ambulation.
b. *Instruct* resident to hold cane in the hand opposite the compromised extremity, that is, the hand on the strong side (Figure 3-2).	Holding the cane on the strong side reduces strain on the compromised extremity since, during usual ambulation, the opposite leg and arm move together.
c. Check the fit of the cane. The cane handle should be at the level of the resident's great trochanter. The resident's elbow should be at a 30-degree angle. The cane should be held six inches lateral to the fifth toe (Figure 3-3).	
d. *Encourage* resident to move the cane forward when the compromised leg is moved forward.	
e. *Encourage* resident to keep the cane close to her/his body and to bear down on the cane when the strong leg begins to move forward.	
f. *Give* resident verbal *encouragement*. Praise efforts and successes.	Acknowledgment of efforts and successes increases the resident's self esteem.
g. Observe the resident's endurance. If the resident becomes weak or very tired, stay with the resident and call for assistance. Use a wheelchair to return resident to a chair or bed.	Continual observation of the resident prevents overexertion.

PROCEDURE	RATIONALE
6. At completion of ambulation, *encourage* resident to *choose* location to rest, e.g., room, lounge, etc.	The ability to choose promotes independence for the resident.
7. Wash your hands.	Hand washing prevents the spread of infection.

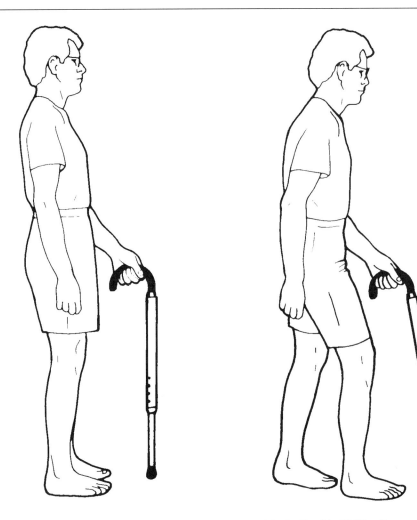

Figure 3-2 Holding the Walking Cane.

Figure 3-3 The Fit of the Walking Cane.

DOCUMENTATION

1. Date and time of ambulation
2. Distance resident ambulated and her/his level of endurance
3. Ability of resident to use cane
4. Any other support/assistance the resident required
5. If ambulation is abruptly stopped due to the resident's intolerance, document the circumstance, a description of the resident (appearance, vital signs), and all nursing action taken
6. Signature and title of nursing staff member

EVALUATION

1. The resident will be safe and physically stable during ambulation.
2. The resident's level of flexibility, balance, strength, and endurance will be gradually increased.
3. The resident will be without areas of skin breakdown.
4. The resident will be actively involved in completion of ADL.

Nursing System

	Wholly Compensatory
✔	Partly Compensatory
✔	Supportive-Educative

AMBULATION WITH WALKER

OBJECTIVES

1. To promote resident's safety and stability during ambulation
2. To increase the resident's level of flexibility, strength, and endurance
3. To increase circulation and minimize the risk of developing skin breakdown
4. To encourage the resident's active involvement in completion of ADL

LEVEL OF RESPONSIBILITY

Registered nurse, licensed practical nurse, certified nursing assistant

POLICY

Each resident who is able to walk will be encouraged to walk and, if necessary, assisted with ambulation at least three times per day.

EQUIPMENT

1. Walker (Figure 3-4)
2. Supportive, comfortable walking shoes for the resident

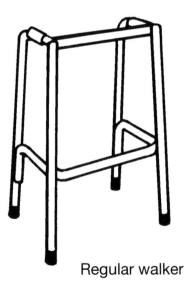

Regular walker

Figure 3-4 The Walker.

PROCEDURE	RATIONALE
1. *Encourage* resident to *choose* the time for ambulation.	The ability to choose promotes independence for the resident.
2. At agreed upon time, *explain* procedure to patient. Focus on ambulation goals for the present ambulation session.	Focusing on goals fosters a sense of progress, achievement, and future for the resident.
3. Wash your hands.	Hand washing prevents the spread of infection.
4. *Encourage* and/or *assist* resident to assume a sitting position and to put on nonskid, supportive footwear.	Proper footwear enhances ambulation ability.
5. Depending on the resident's ability, she/he may need assistance in one or more of the following steps.	
a. *Encourage* resident to assume an upright, standing position in front of the walker. Feet should be planted on the floor, head should be raised and looking forward (Figures 3-5 and 3-6).	An upright position promotes good balance and is imperative to successful ambulation.
b. Resident then lifts the walker with both hands and places it slightly ahead of herself/himself.	
c. Resident takes one or two steps into the walker (Figure 3-7).	
d. Repeat steps *a, b,* and *c.*	
6. Continue ambulation until the agreed upon goal is reached. *Give* resident verbal *encouragement*. Praise efforts and successes.	Acknowledgment of efforts and successes increases the resident's self esteem.
7. Observe the resident's endurance. If resident becomes weak or very tired, stay with the resident and call for assistance. Use a wheelchair to return resident to a chair or bed.	Continual observation of the resident prevents overexertion.
8. At completion of ambulation, *encourage* resident to *choose* location to rest, e.g., room, lounge, etc. *Encourage* resident to back walker to seat (Figure 3-8).	The ability to choose promotes independence for the resident.
9. Wash your hands.	Hand washing prevents the spread of infection.

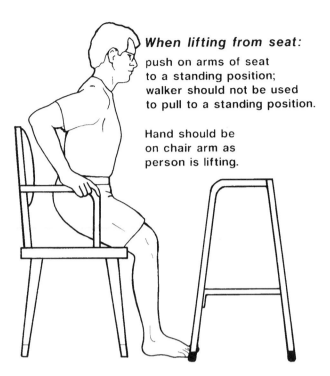

When lifting from seat:
push on arms of seat
to a standing position;
walker should not be used
to pull to a standing position.

Hand should be
on chair arm as
person is lifting.

Figure 3-5 Lifting from Seat to Walker.

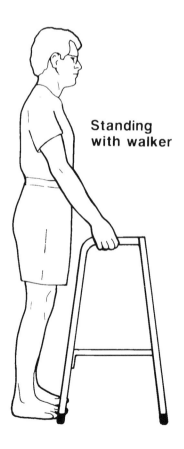

**Standing
with walker**

Figure 3-6 Standing with Walker.

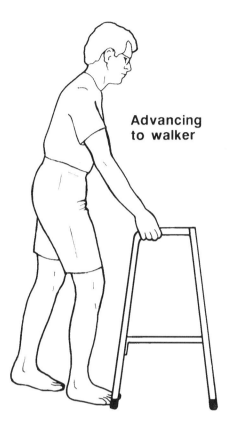

Advancing
to walker

Figure 3-7 Advancing to Walker.

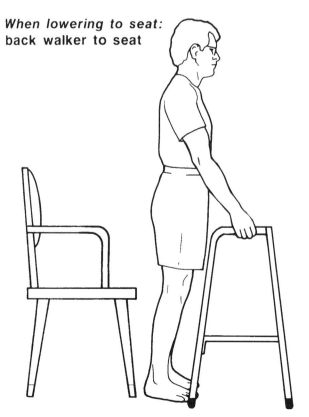

When lowering to seat:
back walker to seat

Figure 3-8 Backing Walker to Seat.

DOCUMENTATION

1. Date and time of ambulation
2. Distance resident ambulated and her/his level of endurance
3. Resident's ability to use walker
4. Any other support/assistance the resident required to ambulate
5. If ambulation is abruptly stopped due to the resident's intolerance, document the circumstance, a description of the resident (appearance, vital signs), and all nursing action taken
6. Signature and title of nursing staff member

EVALUATION

1. The resident will be safe and physically stable during ambulation.
2. The resident's level of flexibility, balance, strength, and endurance will be gradually increased.
3. The resident will be without areas of skin breakdown.
4. The resident will be actively involved in completion of ADL.

Wholly Compensatory
✔ Partly Compensatory
✔ Supportive-Educative

MAINTAINING JOINT MOBILITY (RANGE OF MOTION)

The importance of range of motion in activities of daily living is noted throughout this volume. Maintaining and/or enhancing range of motion promotes the resident's involvement in and completion of activities of daily living. As a result, the resident's independence and level of wellness are enhanced.

OBJECTIVES

1. To promote maximum movement of joints
2. To maintain muscle tone
3. To prevent contractures
4. To stimulate circulation

LEVEL OF RESPONSIBILITY

Registered nurse, licensed practical nurse, certified nursing assistant, physical therapist, physical therapy assistant

POLICY

Active range of motion (ROM) is necessary for daily living. Consult the physician or physical therapist regarding the appropriate level of ROM movements.

PROCEDURE	RATIONALE
1. *Discuss* and *assess* with the resident the need for ROM movements that are not being met by the individual's activities of daily living. Determine any limiting factors.	ROM beyond ADL is contraindicated in the following conditions: a. Septic joints b. Acute thrombophlebitis c. Severe arthritic joint disease d. Recent trauma
2. *Encourage* the resident to *choose* the time for range of motion.	The ability to choose promotes independence for the resident.
3. At agreed upon time, *discuss* and *explain* what the activity will be.	

PROCEDURE	RATIONALE
4. Wash your hands if hands-on assistance or demonstration of technique is anticipated.	Hand washing prevents the spread of infection.
5. *Encourage* resident to move slowly, gently, and to the maximum normal range of motion or before the point of pain. Figures 3-9 through 3-24 illustrate ROM movements.	A joint should never be forced beyond resistance or beyond the point of pain.
6. After completion of the additional activity, assess the resident for comfort, tenderness of muscles, or pain.	
7. Wash your hands.	Hand washing prevents the spread of infection.

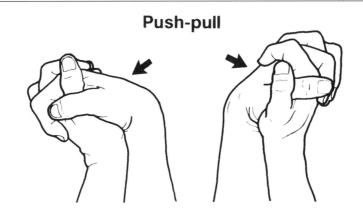

Figure 3-9 Wrist Flexion.

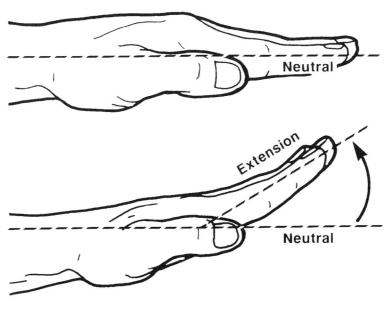

Figure 3-10 Hand and Finger Flexibility.

Shoulder shrugs

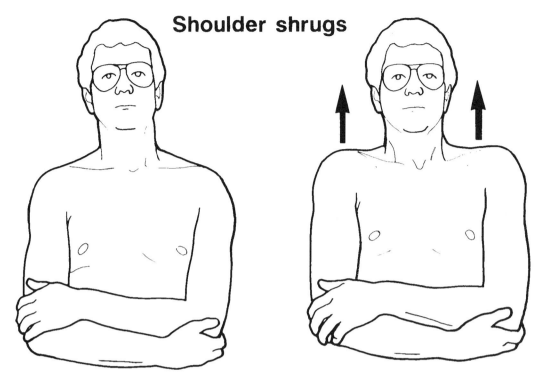

Figure 3-11 Shoulder and Back Muscle Mobility.

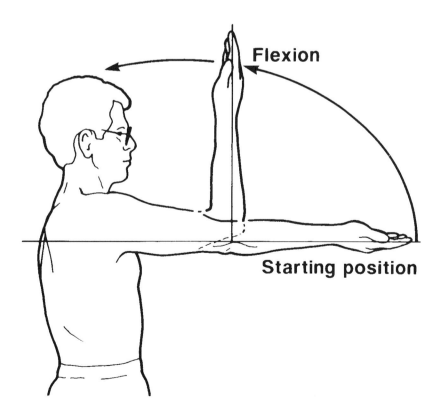

Figure 3-12 Elbow and Bicep Flexion.

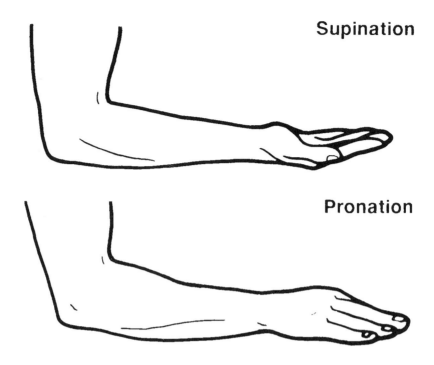

Figure 3-13 Forearm and Wrist Mobility.

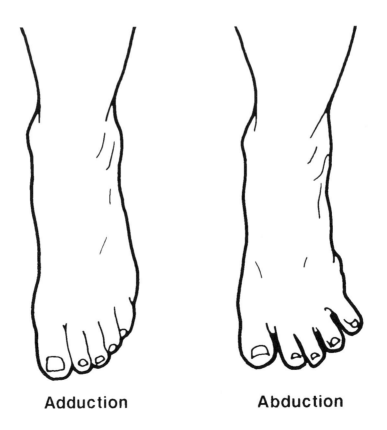

Figure 3-14 Toe and Foot Mobility.

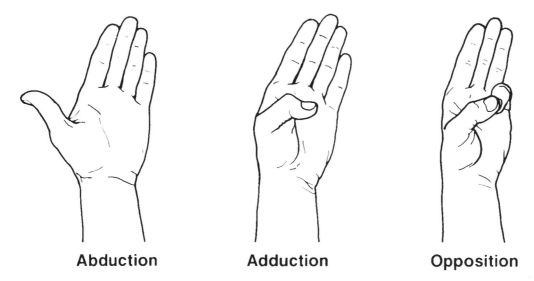

Abduction   **Adduction**   **Opposition**

Figure 3-15 Hand and Finger Dexterity.

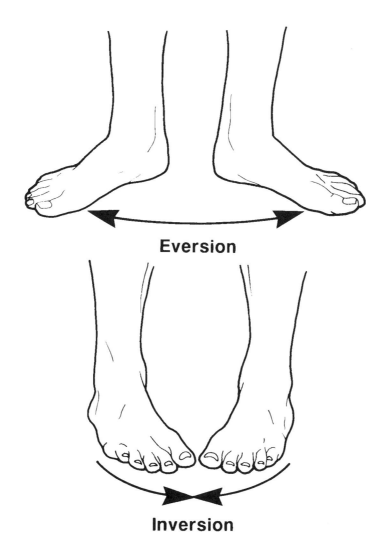

Eversion

Inversion

Figure 3-16 Ankle Mobility and Improved Balance.

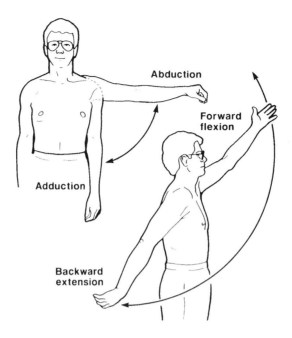

Figure 3-17 Shoulder and Trunk Mobility.

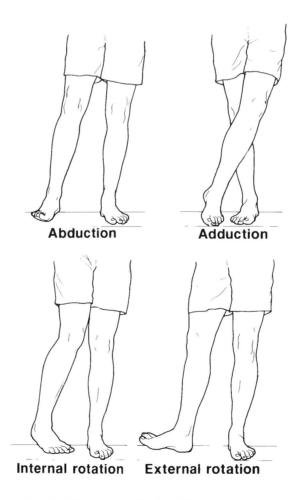

Figure 3-18 Toes, Hip, Ankle, Knee Flexibility. Improved Standing Balance.

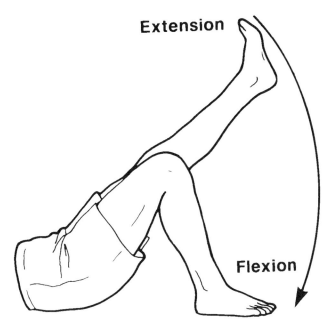

Figure 3-19 Knee and Foot Mobility. Strengthens Abdominal Muscles. Improves Leg Strength.

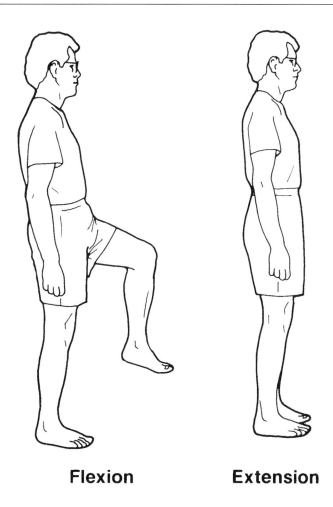

Flexion   **Extension**

Figure 3-20 Knee and Hip Mobility. Improved Balance.

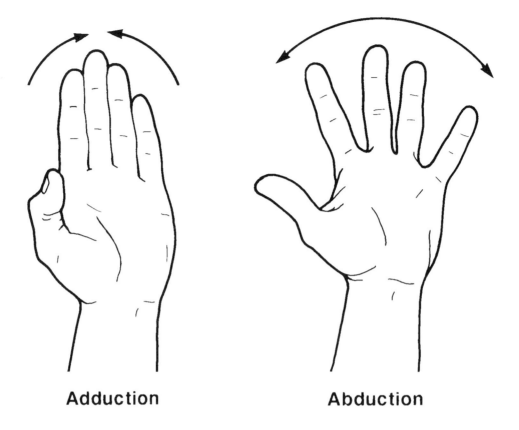

Adduction   **Abduction**

Figure 3-21 Finger and Hand Mobility.

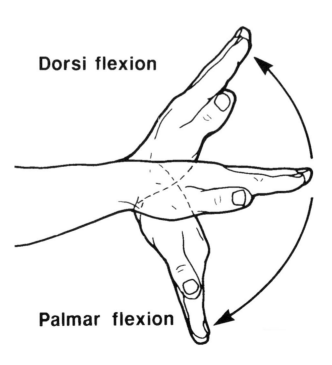

Figure 3-22 Wrist Mobility.

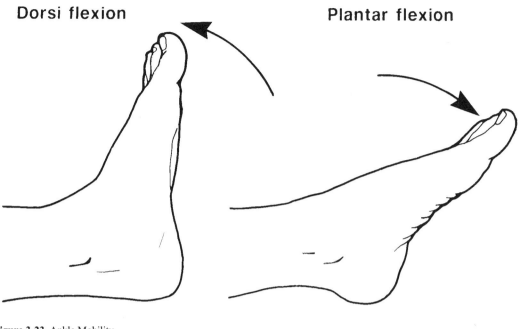

Figure 3-23 Ankle Mobility.

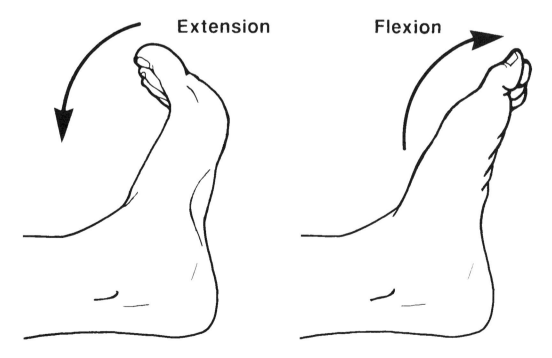

Figure 3-24 Foot and Toe Mobility.

DOCUMENTATION

1. Date and time activity was accomplished
2. Type of movement and position of resident during movement
3. Any complications, resident complaints, and therapeutic effects of exercise
4. Resident's level of participation and reaction to the activity
5. Signature and title of nursing staff member

EVALUATION

1. Resident will maintain maximum range of motion for all joints.
2. Resident will feel the movements are beneficial and therapeutic to his or her overall well-being.
3. Resident will not have complications related to decreased circulation or contracture of muscles due to lack of movement.

	Wholly Compensatory
✔	Partly Compensatory
✔	Supportive-Educative

STANDING

OBJECTIVES

1. To increase the resident's level of strength and endurance
2. To increase circulation and minimize the risk of developing skin breakdown
3. To encourage the resident's active involvement in completion of ADL

LEVEL OF RESPONSIBILITY

Registered nurse, licensed practical nurse, certified nursing assistant

EQUIPMENT

Supportive, comfortable walking shoes for the resident

PROCEDURE	RATIONALE
1. *Encourage* resident to *choose* time for ambulation.	The ability to choose promotes independence for the resident.
2. Wash your hands.	Hand washing prevents the spread of infection.
3. *Encourage* resident to assume a sitting position and to put on nonskid supportive footwear.	Proper footwear enhances safety.
4. If resident requires assistance with assuming an upright, standing position, *offer assistance* using the following steps:	
a. Face the resident.	
b. Grasp onto each side of the resident's rib cage.	
c. Push your knee against one of the resident's knees.	Knee contact promotes safety and fosters the ability of the nurse and resident to work as a unit.
d. Rock the resident to a standing position. Your knee and the resident's knee continue to be pushing against each other.	

PROCEDURE	RATIONALE
e. Be certain that the resident's knees are fully extended.	Full knee extension promotes good balance.
f. Ascertain the resident's ability to balance by self before beginning next activity, e.g., pivoting into chair, using walker, etc.	
5. Wash your hands.	Hand washing prevents the spread of infection.

DOCUMENTATION

1. Date and time of standing activity
2. Duration of standing activity
3. If applicable, the resident's ability to begin the next activity, e.g., use walker
4. Amount of support/assistance the resident required
5. Signature and title of nursing staff member

EVALUATION

1. The resident's level of strength and endurance will be gradually increased.
2. The resident will be without areas of skin breakdown.
3. The resident will be actively involved in completion of ADL.

chapter 4

Eating

Nursing System

✔ Wholly Compensatory
✔ Partly Compensatory
✔ Supportive-Educative

EATING

OBJECTIVES

1. To encourage adequate oral intake
2. To encourage resident's active involvement in completion of ADL

LEVEL OF RESPONSIBILITY

Registered nurse, licensed practical nurse, certified nursing assistant

PROCEDURE	RATIONALE
1. *Encourage* resident's readiness for daily meals, i.e., hands washed, oral care maintained. If possible, *encourage* resident to *choose* time for meals or snacks.	The resident's readiness for meals and ability to choose promotes independence and encourages oral intake.
2. Wash your hands.	Hand washing prevents the spread of infection.
3. *Encourage* and, if necessary, *assist* resident to:	

PROCEDURE	RATIONALE
a. Ambulate to dining room if mobile. b. Transfer to chair in dining room if resident has limited mobility.	Eating in the dining room facilitates a sense of community, maintains a lifelong pattern of eating with others, and stimulates appetite.
4. *Encourage* resident to be as independent as possible during the eating activity. If the resident requires assistance, *help* as needed using the following sequence: a. Arrange a napkin on the resident's lap. b. Open containers. c. Verbally *encourage* resident's use of cup and/or utensils. If resident is unable to feed self, select food item based on resident's preference and feed resident a small amount of food with each bite. d. Take time with feeding resident. Allow time to chew thoroughly. Talk to resident pleasantly during meals. e. *Encourage* and, if necessary, *assist* with oral care and washing hands and face after meals.	Independence in the eating activity maintains personal intactness and autonomy. It also promotes adequate mastication and digestion.
5. Wash your hands.	Hand washing prevents the spread of infection.

DOCUMENTATION

1. Date, time, and amount of food resident ate during the meal
2. Type of diet served
3. Amount and type of eating activity resident was able to independently complete
4. Signature and title of nursing staff member

EVALUATION

1. The resident will consume an adequate oral intake to maintain her/his normal, average weight
2. The resident will be actively involved in completion of ADL.

chapter 5

Continence

Nursing System

	Wholly Compensatory
✔	Partly Compensatory
✔	Supportive-Educative

CATHETER—EXTERNAL (TEXAS)

OBJECTIVES

1. To provide a dry environment for incontinent male residents
2. To prevent skin irritation
3. To encourage resident's active involvement in completion of ADL

LEVEL OF RESPONSIBILITY

Registered nurse, licensed practical nurse

POLICY

Catheter should be changed each day. Release of tape and assessment of circulation should be performed every 8 hours.

EQUIPMENT

1. External catheter kit
2. Soap and water
3. Washcloth and towel
4. Nonsterile gloves

PROCEDURE	**RATIONALE**
1. *Encourage* the resident to *choose* the time for the catheter change.	The ability to choose promotes independence for the resident.
2. At agreed upon time, gather equipment and bring to bedside.	
3. *Explain* procedure to the resident and provide privacy for the activity.	
4. Wash your hands.	Hand washing prevents the spread of infection.
5. *Ask* resident to assume a Fowler's position (see Appendix B). Drape resident to expose genitalia only. Avoid unnecessary exposure.	
6. *Encourage* resident to do as much of the procedure for himself as possible. This could be any or all parts of the catheter change activity.	Self performance of the activity promotes independence and self esteem.
7. Put on gloves if nursing staff is assisting with any portion of the procedure.	Use of gloves protects both the resident and the nurse and prevents the spread of infection.
8. *Encourage* resident to wash penis and perineal area with soap and water. Dry thoroughly. If resident is not circumcised, retract foreskin to cleanse the glans. Gently ease foreskin back into place after drying.	This prevents skin irritation or breakdown.
9. Coat shaft of penis with skin prep (found in catheter kit). Allow skin to dry.	Skin prep allows more stable contact between catheter and skin.
10. Roll external catheter over penis. Leave a reservoir of 1 to 2 inches between the end of the penis and connecting tube.	This avoids pressure to the glans.
11. Secure the external catheter firmly, but not tightly, about $^3/_4$ to 1 inch from the base of the penis with the tape provided. The tape should completely encircle the penis without covering the edge of the external catheter completely or covering the skin with the tape.	Improper application of the device can result in impaired circulation. Tape may damage the external catheter causing leakage or may irritate delicate skin of the penis.
12. Connect external catheter to drainage bag (see Figure 5-1).	
13. Check catheter for patency and inspect skin every 8 hours. Check for irritation, discoloration, and leakage of urine around the penis or bag.	

PROCEDURE	RATIONALE
14. Ask resident to report irritation, discoloration, or leakage to nursing staff.	This promotes independence and participation in self care.
15. Discard disposable items appropriately.	
16. Wash your hands.	Hand washing prevents the spread of infection.

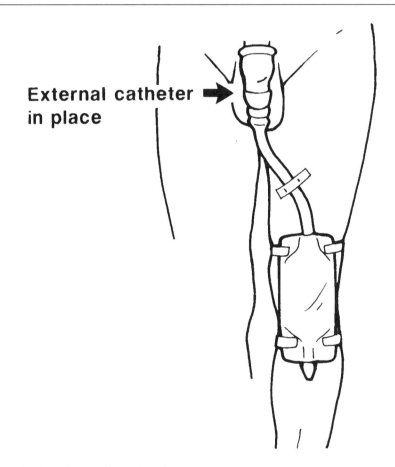

External catheter in place

Figure 5-1 External Catheter Connected to Drainage Bag.

DOCUMENTATION

1. Date and time external catheter was applied
2. Assessment of condition of the penis and drainage system
3. Resident's tolerance of the procedure
4. Amount of self care resident was able to perform
5. Notification of the physician of any unusual swelling, redness, irritation, etc.
6. Any teaching done and resident's level of understanding
7. Signature and title of nursing staff

EVALUATION

1. Resident will understand the need for use of the external catheter.
2. Resident will understand that signs and symptoms of irritation, leakage, or loss of sensation must be reported to nursing staff immediately.
3. Resident will be able to participate in self performance of procedure.

INSERTION OF CATHETER—SUPRAPUBIC

OBJECTIVES

1. To maintain constant urinary drainage when urinary tract is obstructed
2. To encourage resident's active involvement in completion of ADL

LEVEL OF RESPONSIBILITY

Physician, registered nurse, licensed practical nurse

POLICY

Change catheter only upon order of the physician.

EQUIPMENT

1. Sterile catheter insertion set
2. Sterile indwelling catheter of the size and type ordered by the physician
3. Sterile water
4. Sterile gloves

PROCEDURE	RATIONALE
1. If compatible with physician's orders, *encourage* resident to *choose* the time for catheter change.	The ability to choose promotes independence for the resident.
2. Check physician's order before catheter change.	
3. Gather equipment and bring to bedside.	
4. Wash your hands.	Hand washing prevents the spread of infection.
5. *Explain* each step of the procedure to the resident. *Encourage* resident to ask questions and express any feelings about the procedure.	Involvement in the procedure reinforces independence and self esteem.
6. *Encourage* and *assist* resident to assume a supine position (see Appendix B) and drape for privacy.	

PROCEDURE	RATIONALE
7. Open sterile catheter insertion set.	
8. Peel back wrapper of catheter. Place catheter on sterile working surface. Do not contaminate contents.	This is a sterile procedure.
9. Put on sterile gloves.	
10. Place protective pad below opening for catheter.	
11. Place sterile drape as close as possible to opening for catheter.	
12. Open lubricating jelly and squeeze onto catheter tip.	
13. Using a clean cotton ball for each cleansing, swab with antiseptic solution. Begin at edges of opening and cleanse in concentric circles moving outward.	
14. Clean directly over opening with last cotton ball and antiseptic solution, taking care not to let solution run into opening.	This provides an aseptic site for catheter insertion.
15. *Encourage* resident to notify nursing staff of tenderness at insertion site or surrounding area.	
16. Gently, without force, insert lubricated catheter into opening about 1 to $1^{1}/_{2}$ inches until urine flows into catheter. Note: If any difficulty or resistance is encountered, stop. Withdraw catheter. Call physician.	
17. Place opposite end of catheter into specimen container if specimen is required.	
18. After specimen is obtained, inflate balloon with sterile water to capacity indicated on catheter or according to physician's orders.	
19. Attach catheter to drainage bag.	
20. Properly position bag below level of bladder. (Bag must not touch floor.)	Placing bag below level of bladder encourages flow of urine. Avoid contact of bag with floor to prevent contamination of drainage system.
21. If bedbound, secure bag to bed frame (never to side rail).	Movement of the side rail may displace catheter from insertion site.

PROCEDURE	RATIONALE
22. Apply 4 by 4 inch dressing that has been slit from one end to center of bandage.	This allows close contact application of dressing around catheter to ensure cleanliness in the area.
23. Discard disposable equipment properly.	
24. Wash your hands.	Hand washing prevents the spread of infection.

DOCUMENTATION

1. Date and time of procedure
2. Amount of urine (if specimen was obtained), color and consistency of urine
3. Condition of the orifice and skin surrounding orifice
4. Resident's tolerance and understanding of the procedure
5. Type of dressing applied
6. Signature and title of nursing staff member

EVALUATION

1. Resident will understand the purpose for the procedure.
2. Resident will remain free of infection at insertion site.
3. Resident's skin will not become excoriated or irritated.

Nursing System

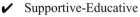

	Wholly Compensatory
✔	Partly Compensatory
✔	Supportive-Educative

CARE OF CATHETER—SUPRAPUBIC

OBJECTIVES

1. To maintain clean catheter insertion site
2. To maintain catheter patency
3. To encourage resident's active involvement in completion of ADL

LEVEL OF RESPONSIBILITY

Registered nurse, licensed practical nurse

POLICY

Care should be provided each day and as often as necessary.

EQUIPMENT

1. Soap
2. Washcloth and towel
3. Nonsterile gloves

PROCEDURE	RATIONALE
1. Check physician's orders for specific catheter care instructions.	
2. *Encourage* the resident to *choose* the time for catheter care.	The ability to choose promotes independence for the resident.
3. Gather equipment and bring to bedside.	
4. *Explain* procedure to resident and screen for privacy.	
5. *Encourage* and *assist* resident to assume a supine position (see Appendix B). Drape for privacy.	
6. Wash your hands.	Hand washing prevents the spread of infection.
7. *Encourage* resident to do as much of the procedure for self as possible. This could	Self performance of catheter care activities promotes independence.

PROCEDURE	RATIONALE
be any or all parts of the catheter care activity, from applying soap on the washcloth to complete catheter care.	
8. Put on gloves if nursing staff member is performing any portion of the following procedure.	Use of gloves protects both the resident and the nurse and prevents the spread of infection.
9. First, clean any crusted material from catheter insertion site.	This avoids contaminated material from area around catheter being introduced into insertion site.
10. Clean area around catheter with warm water and soap applied to washcloth.	
11. Rinse and dry area well.	
12. *Encourage* resident to report to nursing staff any discomfort at insertion site or surrounding area.	This reinforces resident involvement in self care and promotes independence.
13. Clean and return reusable equipment to proper area.	
14. Wash your hands.	Hand washing prevents the spread of infection.

DOCUMENTATION

1. Date and time of procedure
2. Condition of skin around catheter, noting presence of reddened or irritated areas or drainage at the insertion site
3. Drainage quantity, color, odor
4. Patency of catheter
5. Amount of self care resident was able to perform
6. Resident's level of understanding of procedure
7. Signature and title of nursing staff member

EVALUATION

1. Resident's skin will be free of irritation or drainage at insertion site.
2. Catheter will remain patent with free flow of urine.
3. Resident will understand the need to keep the catheter and insertion site clean to prevent infection.
4. Resident will assist in self-care process.

	Wholly Compensatory
✔	Partly Compensatory
✔	Supportive-Educative

CATHETER CARE (HYGIENIC MANAGEMENT)

OBJECTIVES

1. To prevent infection
2. To reduce irritation
3. To encourage resident's active involvement in completion of ADL

LEVEL OF RESPONSIBILITY

Registered nurse, licensed practical nurse, certified nursing assistant

POLICY

Catheter care shall be provided to residents daily and as often as needed thereafter.

EQUIPMENT

1. Basin with warm water and soap
2. Towel and washcloth
3. Nonsterile gloves
4. Bedpan
5. Disposable container for measuring urine

PROCEDURE	RATIONALE
1. *Encourage* the resident to *choose* the time for catheter care.	The ability to choose promotes independence for the resident.
2. At agreed upon time, *explain* the procedure to the resident and bring equipment to the resident's room.	
3. Wash your hands.	Hand washing prevents the spread of infection.
4. *Encourage* the resident to attain a semi-Fowler's position (see Appendix B) on bedpan if bedbound. If resident is ambulatory, *assist* to the bathroom or to the commode.	

PROCEDURE	RATIONALE
5. Arrange equipment within easy reach of the resident and *encourage* resident to *assist* with the cleansing procedure as much as possible. This could involve any or all parts of the cleansing activity, from applying soap on the washcloth to the entire catheter care procedure.	Self performance of catheter care promotes independence and encourages exercise, range of motion, and good hygiene habits.
6. Put on gloves if assisting with procedure.	Use of gloves protects both the resident and nurse and prevents the spread of infection.
7. If the resident is incontinent of stool and has had a bowel movement, clean this area first. If the nurse is assisting, apply clean gloves and obtain clean equipment to continue care.	
8. Wash perineum well with soap and warm water. *Explain* to the resident the need to wash perineum front to back to prevent fecal contamination at catheter insertion site.	Risk of contamination is increased by washing perineum back to front because of the possibility of introducing fecal material or bacteria to the urethral area.
9. Cleanse area at catheter insertion site well with soap and warm water. Take care not to pull on the catheter or advance it further into the urethra.	
10. Remove all debris from the catheter at insertion site.	
11. Rinse area well with warm water. Gently pat dry with clean towel.	
12. Empty urine into disposable container from exit port on the bag. Measure and observe urine carefully.	Accurate measurement is essential for intake/ output records. Urine should be observed for cloudiness, odor, or debris as this may indicate an infectious process that must be reported to the physician.
13. Discard disposable equipment properly.	
14. Place linen in appropriate container.	
15. Empty, clean, and store bedpan if used.	
16. Wash your hands.	Hand washing prevents the spread of infection.

DOCUMENTATION

1. Date and time of procedure
2. Condition of the perineum and catheter insertion site, noting any redness, irritation, or excoriation
3. Color, consistency, amount, and odor of urine (also documented on intake/output record if ordered by physician)
4. Amount of self care the resident was able to perform
5. Resident's tolerance of the procedure
6. Signature and title of nursing staff

EVALUATION

1. Resident will understand the importance of catheter care to prevent infection and irritation.
2. Resident will understand the importance of catheter care to maintain good hygiene.
3. Resident will be able to contribute to the self-care process.

Nursing System

✔ Wholly Compensatory Partly Compensatory Supportive-Educative

CATHETERIZATION—INDWELLING

OBJECTIVES

1. To permit urinary drainage for neurogenic bladder conditions or urinary retention problems
2. To relieve urinary tract obstruction problems
3. To empty urine from the bladder following bladder, prostate, or vaginal surgery

LEVEL OF RESPONSIBILITY

Registered nurse, licensed practical nurse

POLICY

Indwelling catheters are placed only on order of the physician. Always use the smallest size catheter capable of providing adequate drainage. Replacement of permanent catheters is usually every 30 to 60 days.

EQUIPMENT

1. Sterile catheterization kit
2. Sterile drainage tubing and collection bag
3. Sterile catheter of the size ordered by the physician
4. Tape or leg strap if required
5. Disposable bag
6. Flashlight or lamp, if needed

PROCEDURE	RATIONALE
1. If compatible with physician's orders, *encourage* resident to *choose* the time for catheter change.	The ability to choose promotes independence for the resident.
2. At agreed upon time, *explain* the procedure and purpose to the resident.	
3. Screen for privacy.	
4. Follow appropriate steps for female or male resident.	

PROCEDURE	RATIONALE

Female

1. *Encourage* and *assist* resident to attain a lithotomy position (see Appendix B).

2. Wash your hands.

   Hand washing prevents the spread of infection.

3. Stand on side of the bed that places your dominant hand to the bottom of the bed.

4. Open catheter kit using aseptic technique. Open package containing drainage bag and tubing using sterile technique as well.

   Catheterization requires strict sterile technique to avoid contamination leading to urinary tract infection.

5. Direct light for visualization of genitalia.

6. Put on sterile gloves found in kit.

   Use of gloves protects both the resident and the nurse and prevents the spread of infection.

7. Place moisture-proof pad (found in kit) under resident's buttocks.

8. With nondominant hand, separate labia minora so that urinary meatus is easily seen (see Figure 5-2). This glove is now considered contaminated and should not touch sterile equipment.

9. Cleanse the area around the urinary meatus with the provided cotton balls soaked in the solution contained in the kit. Always use downward strokes to cleanse the area.

   This avoids accidental contamination of the urethral area by bacteria from the anal area.

10. Lubricate catheter well with lubricant provided in kit.

    Thorough lubrication reduces irritation during insertion.

11. Gently insert catheter into urinary meatus approximately 2 to 3 inches (see Figure 5-3). Urine should begin to flow at this time. Be sure opposite end of catheter is resting on moisture-proof pad or in tray from catheterization kit.

    Urine will begin to flow through tube immediately. Be prepared for spillage before tubing and bag are attached to catheter.

12. If a urine specimen is needed, allow a small amount of urine to flow through catheter before obtaining specimen in sterile container included in kit.

    This avoids using a concentrated sample of urine, which may not yield accurate lab results.

13. Attach tubing and bag to opposite end of catheter. Be sure urine is flowing. Then gently push catheter approximately $1/2$ inch further.

PROCEDURE	RATIONALE
14. Ask resident if there is any discomfort or pain before inflating balloon with normal saline and syringe provided in kit.	Discomfort may indicate that the catheter is inappropriately placed.
15. Inflate balloon as indicated to the amount indicated on kit instructions or as ordered by physician.	
16. After inflating balloon, assess the resident's comfort level. It may be necessary to adjust the position of the catheter by simply rotating it slightly. Or it may be necessary to remove a small amount of saline from the balloon to ensure comfort to the resident.	A smaller amount of saline may be needed if the resident has a smaller than normal bladder due to surgery, medical condition, or age.
17. If resident will be ambulatory, attach leg strap to catheter tubing. Follow instructions on leg strap package. If tape is preferred by the resident, allow approximately 2 inches of slack in the catheter before attaching tape to an area of inner thigh with as little hair as possible.	
18. If resident will remain in bed, hook bag to bed frame below level of the bladder.	This prevents back flow of urine by keeping bag lower than bladder. Also, prevents trauma from catheter being accidentally pulled.
19. Allow the resident to *discuss* any feelings about the procedure and the use of an indwelling catheter.	
20. Observe urine in bag for color, clarity, or blood clots.	
21. Wash your hands.	Hand washing prevents the spread of infection.
22. To remove catheter, withdraw all of saline through the exit port with a syringe or place moisture-proof pad under the exit port and cut the tip off. When all of the saline has been removed, gently guide catheter back out of urinary meatus. Direction will be straight back.	
23. Inspect tip of catheter for encrustation.	Debris collected at tip of catheter may indicate the need for more frequent catheter changes, increased fluid intake, or infectious process. Physician should be notified.

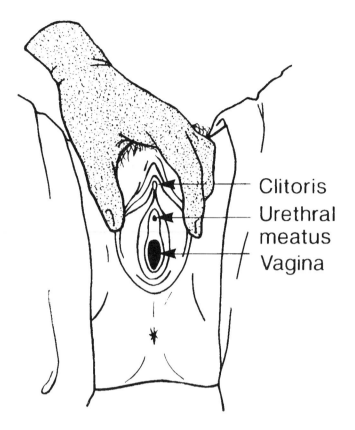

Figure 5-2 Visualizing the Urethral Meatus.

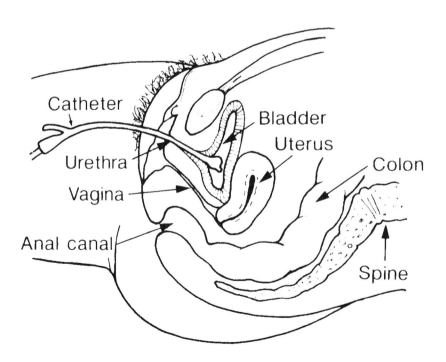

Figure 5-3 Catheter Inserted 2 to 3 Inches To Reach Female Bladder.

PROCEDURE	RATIONALE

Male

1. Follow steps 1 through 6 for female resident except *assist* male resident to a supine position (Appendix B).

2. Place the moisture-proof pad across the resident's upper thighs.

3. Cleanse the area around the urinary meatus and the glans using downward strokes with the cotton balls provided (Figure 5-4).

4. Using the lubricant provided in the kit, lubricate the catheter approximately 1 1/2 inches on the shaft.

   The length of the urethra in the male requires more lubrication to avoid trauma during catheter insertion.

5. Hold the penis at right angle to the resident's body (Figure 5-5).

   This straightens the urethra for ease of insertion.

6. Gently guide catheter approximately 6 to 8 inches into bladder (Figure 5-6). Urine should begin to flow at this time. Be sure opposite end of catheter is resting on moisture-proof pad or in tray from catheterization kit.

   Urine will begin to flow through tube immediately. Be prepared for spillage before tubing and bag are attached to catheter.

7. Continue with steps 12 through 21 as for female resident.

8. To remove catheter, withdraw all of saline through the exit port with a syringe or place moisture-proof pad under the exit port and cut the tip off. When all of the saline has been removed, hold penis at right angle to the body and gently extract catheter in an upward motion.

9. Inspect tip of catheter for encrustation.

   Debris collected at tip of catheter may indicate the need for more frequent catheter changes, increased fluid intake, or infectious process. Physician should be notified.

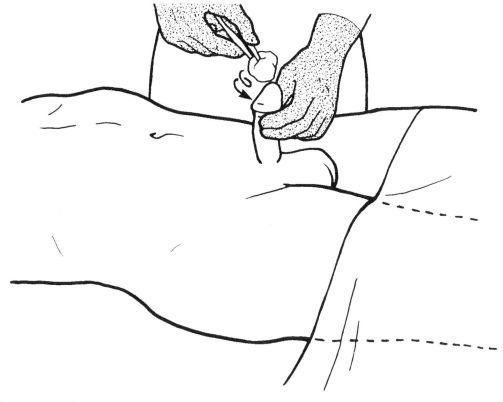

Figure 5-4 Cleansing the Urinary Meatus and Glans.

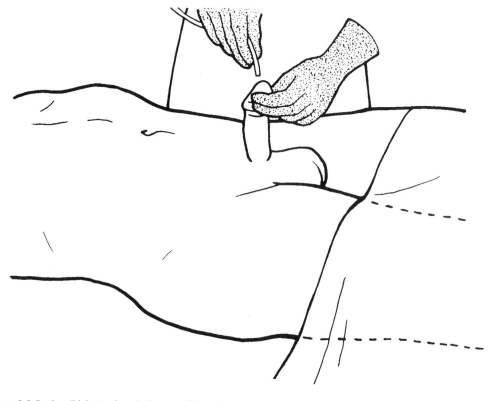

Figure 5-5 Penis at Right Angle to Body To Straighten Urethra.

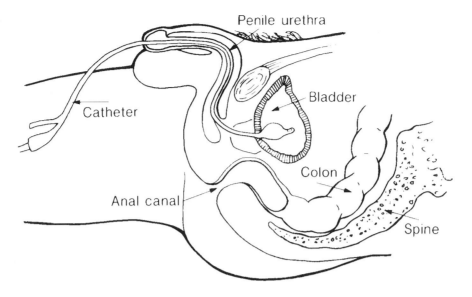

Figure 5-6 Catheter Inserted 6 to 8 Inches To Reach Male Bladder.

DOCUMENTATION

1. Date and time of catheterization
2. Color, consistency, amount, and odor of urine (also documented on intake/output record if ordered by physician)
3. Resident's feelings about catheterization
4. Any indications of encrustation or infection and, if so, action taken
5. Signature and title of nursing staff member

EVALUATION

1. Resident will not have urinary retention.
2. Resident will feel comfortable with catheter in place.
3. Resident will be able to discuss feelings related to the indwelling catheter.
4. There will be no indication of infection caused by the catheter.

CATHETERIZATION—INTERMITTENT

OBJECTIVES

1. To promote reflex bladder functioning as part of a bladder retraining program
2. To prevent distention and overfilling of the bladder
3. To reduce the incidence of urinary tract infections and other problems associated with long-term use of an indwelling catheter
4. To encourage resident's active involvement in completion of ADL

LEVEL OF RESPONSIBILITY

Registered nurse, licensed practical nurse

POLICY

Perform catheterization every 6 to 8 hours or as ordered by physician.

EQUIPMENT

1. Soap and warm water
2. Washcloth and towel
3. Nonsterile gloves
4. No. 14 French catheter
5. Water soluble lubricant and shallow basin
6. Mirror (female patient)
7. Fluid intake/output record

PROCEDURE	RATIONALE
1. If compatible with physician's orders, *encourage* resident to *choose* the time for catheterization.	The ability to choose promotes independence for the resident.
2. At agreed upon time, *explain* procedure and purpose to resident.	
3. If resident is bedbound, bring equipment to bedside. If resident is ambulatory, *assist* to the bathroom or commode.	
4. Wash your hands.	Hand washing prevents the spread of infection.

PROCEDURE	RATIONALE
5. Put on gloves if assisting with any portion of the procedure.	Use of gloves protects both the resident and the nurse and prevents the spread of infection.
6. If resident is unable to void and if in the nursing staff's judgment, the resident is more secure in bed, *assist* resident to attain a semi-Fowler's position (see Appendix B).	
7. If resident is able to ambulate to the bathroom or commode, *assist* to a comfortable position.	
8. *Encourage* resident to attempt to void using stimulation techniques as indicated (i.e., running water, warm towel on abdomen, or stroking inner thigh).	This stimulates reflex bladder functioning at scheduled time.
9. *Encourage* resident to do as much for self as possible. This could be any or all parts of the catheterization procedure.	Self performance of catheterization promotes independence and self esteem.
10. Cleanse the urinary meatus with soap and warm water.	
11. Catheterize resident or *guide* resident in self catheterization using clean technique.	Sterile technique is necessary in the hospital setting only.
12. Follow appropriate steps for female or male resident.	

Female

1. Lubricate catheter tip.

2. Position mirror for resident to visualize urinary meatus.

3. Guide lubricated catheter gently into the meatus. Allow urine to flow into shallow pan.

4. Gently guide catheter back out of meatus. Direction will be straight back.

5. Measure the amount of urine removed from the bladder.

6. Notify physician if volumes obtained are consistently greater than 300 cubic centimeters or once voluntary micturition has resumed.	Large volume may indicate the need to increase the frequency of catheterization. Physician should be notified.

PROCEDURE	RATIONALE
7. *Assist* resident to attain a comfortable position after catheterization. Allow resident time to *discuss* any feelings about the procedure and/or self performance of the procedure.	
8. Wash your hands.	Hand washing prevents the spread of infection.

Male

1. Lubricate catheter approximately 1½ inches on shaft.	The length of the urethra in the male requires more lubrication to avoid trauma during catheter insertion.
2. Hold penis at right angle to resident's body.	This straightens the urethra for ease of insertion.
3. Gently guide catheter approximately 6 to 8 inches into bladder. Allow urine to flow into shallow pan.	
4. With penis held at right angle to body, gently extract catheter in an upward motion.	
5. Continue with steps 5 through 8 as for female resident.	

DOCUMENTATION

1. Date and time of catheterization
2. Color, consistency, amount, and odor of urine (also documented on intake/output record if ordered by physician)
3. Amount of self care resident was able to perform
4. Signature and title of nursing staff member

EVALUATION

1. Resident will establish reflex bladder functioning.
2. Resident will be able to perform some if not all, of the catheterization procedure.
3. Resident will not have a urinary tract infection or become distended.
4. Resident will understand the need for the procedure and participate in the retraining steps as needed.

Nursing System

| ✔ | Wholly Compensatory |
Partly Compensatory
Supportive-Educative

ENEMA—CLEANSING

OBJECTIVES

1. To stimulate defecation in the treatment of constipation
2. To help establish regular bowel function during a bowel retraining program
3. To encourage resident's active involvement in completion of ADL

LEVEL OF RESPONSIBILITY

Registered nurse, licensed practical nurse, certified nursing assistant

POLICY

Cleansing enemas are given as needed to relieve constipation. Occasionally they are given daily to establish regular bowel function, if ordered by the physician.

EQUIPMENT

1. Disposable enema administration set
2. Water soluble lubricant
3. Tap water warmed to 105 to 115 degrees Fahrenheit (40.5 to 46 degrees Celsius)
4. Waterproof bed protector
5. Bedpan or bedside commode
6. Nonsterile gloves
7. Towel, washcloth, and toilet tissue
8. Bath blanket

PROCEDURE	RATIONALE
1. *Encourage* resident to *choose* the time for the enema.	The ability to choose promotes independence for the resident.
2. At agreed upon time, bring all equipment to the bedside.	
3. Provide privacy for the resident. *Explain* procedure.	
4. Wash your hands.	Hand washing prevents the spread of infection.
5. Put on gloves.	Use of gloves protects both the resident and the nurse and prevents the spread of infection.

PROCEDURE	RATIONALE
6. Place 32 ounces of warm tap water into enema bag. Add castile soap only if ordered by the physician.	Physician may prefer warm water only.
7. Place waterproof pad under resident's buttocks.	
8. *Assist* resident to a left side lying position with right knee flexed (see Appendix B).	This position follows the natural course of the rectum and colon.
9. Drape for privacy with the bath blanket, exposing only the buttocks.	
10. Hang enema bag on hook or IV pole approximately 12 to 18 inches above anus.	
11. Open clamp of administration kit and allow air to escape from tubing. Reclamp tube.	This prevents cramping caused by introduction of air into the lower bowel.
12. Lubricate tubing approximately 3 to 5 inches.	
13. *Encourage* resident to take deep breaths during insertion.	This relaxes abdominal muscles.
14. Unclamp tubing. Allow fluid to flow slowly. Administration should take about 10 minutes. Allow 500 to 750 milliliters of fluid to flow.	
15. After solution is instilled, clamp and remove tubing.	
16. After removing tubing, hold buttocks together with several layers of toilet tissue for 2 to 3 minutes.	This encourages distension of the colon to hold liquid and facilitate defecation.
17. *Encourage* resident to remain in same position for 10 to 15 minutes.	This gains maximum benefit from the procedure.
18. *Assist* resident onto toilet, commode, or bedpan.	Natural positioning enhances effective defecation.
19. Provide privacy for resident. Be sure call light is within reach or staff member is within calling distance.	Ensuring privacy enhances effective defecation.
20. When defecation is completed, *assist* resident to use soap, water, and towel to clean perineal area. *Assist* resident as needed.	

PROCEDURE	RATIONALE
21. Discard disposable equipment properly. Clean reusable items and return to designated area.	
22. Wash your hands.	Hand washing prevents the spread of infection.
23. If enema is being given as part of a bowel retraining program, *discuss* with the resident the introduction of high fiber foods into the diet, unless contraindicated. *Encourage* eight 8-ounce glasses of fluid every 24 hours if not contraindicated. Also, prune juice may be added one to two times a day if diet permits.	

DOCUMENTATION

1. Date and time of procedure
2. Amount of solution administered
3. Approximate amount, color, and consistency of return
4. Resident's tolerance of procedure
5. Amount of self care resident was able to perform
6. All teaching provided and resident's level of understanding
7. Signature and title of nursing staff member

EVALUATION

1. Lower bowel will be cleansed.
2. Resident will tolerate the procedure without trauma.
3. Resident will understand the need for the procedure and be able to participate in the self-care process.
4. Any suggested dietary changes will be understood by the resident and altered to accommodate specific tastes.

ENEMA—RETENTION

OBJECTIVES

1. To administer medication
2. To soften feces for ease of bowel elimination
3. To assist as part of a bowel retraining program
4. To encourage resident's active involvement in completion of ADL

LEVEL OF RESPONSIBILITY

Registered nurse, licensed practical nurse, certified nursing assistant

POLICY

Retention enemas are given only on order of the physician, using the solution prescribed.

EQUIPMENT

1. Disposable enema administration set
2. Water soluble lubricant
3. Prescribed solution warmed to 105 to 115 degrees Fahrenheit (40.5 to 46 degrees Celsius)
4. Waterproof bed protector
5. Bedpan or bedside commode
6. Towel and washcloth
7. Nonsterile gloves
8. Bath blanket

PROCEDURE	RATIONALE
1. *Encourage* resident to *choose* the time for the enema.	The ability to choose promotes independence for the resident.
2. At agreed upon time, bring all equipment to bedside.	
3. Provide privacy for the resident. *Explain* procedure.	
4. Wash your hands.	Hand washing prevents the spread of infection.

PROCEDURE	RATIONALE
5. Put on gloves.	Use of gloves protects both the resident and the nurse and prevents the spread of infection.
6. Prepare solution as prescribed by the physician.	
7. *Assist* resident to left side lying position with right knee flexed (see Appendix B).	This position follows the natural course of the rectum and colon.
8. Drape for privacy, exposing only the buttocks.	
9. Place waterproof bed protector under resident's buttocks.	
10. Open clamp of administration kit and allow air to escape from tubing. Reclamp tube.	This prevents cramping caused by introduction of air into lower bowel.
11. Lubricate tubing approximately 3 to 5 inches from tip.	
12. Insert tube into rectum approximately 2 to 4 inches. *Encourage* resident to take deep breaths during insertion.	This relaxes abdominal muscles and increases the ability to retain fluid.
13. Hold enema bag approximately 18 inches above anus.	
14. Unclamp the tubing, allow fluid to flow slowly.	
15. If resident expresses a desire to expel the fluid, stop the flow until the desire to evacuate has passed.	
16. After solution is instilled, clamp and remove tubing. Leave small amount of solution in tubing.	Using the entire amount of solution may introduce air into the colon.
17. After removing tubing, hold buttocks together for a few minutes.	Removal of the tubing stimulates the urge to defecate.
18. *Instruct* resident to remain in same position for at least 15 to 30 minutes.	
19. Cover resident with bath blanket. *Encourage* resident to divert attention during waiting period, such as to television or deep breathing.	
20. Ask resident if you should stay during this waiting period to encourage concentration on other subjects.	This encourages decision making affecting the resident's health care and promotes independence and self esteem.

PROCEDURE	RATIONALE
21. After appropriate period of time, *assist* resident to bedpan, commode, or toilet. If resident uses toilet, *instruct* not to flush.	This allows nurse to assess results of procedure.
22. When defecation is completed, *assist* resident to use soap, water, and towel to clean perineal area. *Assist* resident as needed.	
23. Discard disposable equipment properly. Clean reusable items and return to designated area.	
24. Wash your hands.	Hand washing prevents the spread of infection.

DOCUMENTATION

1. Date and time of procedure
2. Amount of solution administered
3. Approximate amount, color, and consistency of return
4. Resident's tolerance of procedure
5. Amount of self care resident was able to perform
6. All teaching provided and resident's level of understanding
7. Signature and title of nursing staff member

EVALUATION

1. Resident will receive medication as ordered.
2. Resident will establish regular pattern of evacuation.
3. Resident will be able to participate in self care.
4. Resident will understand the need for and reasons for the procedure.

Nursing System

✔ Wholly Compensatory
✔ Partly Compensatory
✔ Supportive-Educative

URINARY INCONTINENCE—ASSESSMENT AND INTERVENTIONS

OBJECTIVES

1. To identify possible reasons for urinary incontinence
2. To promote and maintain the resident's regular urination pattern
3. To maintain the resident's overall hygiene and self esteem
4. To encourage the resident's active involvement in completion of ADL

LEVEL OF RESPONSIBILITY

Registered nurse, licensed practical nurse

POLICY

Each resident experiencing urinary incontinence will be examined physically and functionally to identify possible reasons for incontinence and appropriate interventions. This policy and procedure describes the areas of assessment and possible interventions under the procedure column. The rationale column describes reasons for examining these areas and for advocating and providing the interventions.

PROCEDURE	RATIONALE
1. The nurse will *advocate* for appropriate physical evaluation. This will include physician collaboration to consider the following:	
a. Obtain a urine specimen.	Urinary tract infections may cause incontinence.
b. Examine recent bowel movement pattern and check for fecal impaction, if appropriate.	Numerous days without a bowel movement and, often, the occurrence of liquid stool may indicate fecal impaction, which may cause urinary incontinence.
c. Obtain urologic evaluation to help identify other causes for urinary incontinence.	Results of a thorough urologic evaluation will delineate specific interventions that may improve or eliminate the incontinence.
2. Utilize a wet/dry checklist to identify the resident's pattern of urine elimination.	

PROCEDURE	RATIONALE
a. Each hour of the day, check the resident's use of the commode or whether she/he has had an incontinence episode.	
b. Keep a log of this information to determine the frequency with which the resident uses the commode successfully and the amount and timing of incontinence episodes between commode voidings.	Frequent incontinence episodes between commode voidings may indicate the need for more opportunities to use the commode.
c. *Encourage* more frequent use of the commode during incontinence episodes and observe the effect on the wet/dry checklist. Continue to modify commode use as the checklist indicates.	
3. Conduct an environmental assessment to identify factors in the environment that may contribute to the resident's incontinence. An environmental assessment includes the following:	
a. Resident's accessibility to toilet facilities. Are there obstacles to getting to the toilet?	
b. Is the commode of proper height for resident use?	
c. Can the resident disrobe appropriately for commode use?	
d. If the resident wears glasses, are they on?	Visual abilities facilitate bathroom use.
e. Are physical restraints being used?	
4. Examine medications that may affect incontinence. Consult with physician regarding any modifications that may decrease incontinence episodes.	Use of diuretics, hypnotics, or anticholinergic drugs may affect incontinence. Often a change in administration time may alter incontinence. For example, administration of diuretics in the morning may decrease incontinence episodes during the night.
5. *Promote* skin care and self care with incontinent residents. Following are ways to encourage appropriate skin care and self care.	Promotion of self care encourages the resident's feelings of autonomy and control when regular urinary functioning is out of control.

PROCEDURE	RATIONALE
a. *Encourage* frequent perineal care. (See perineal care policy and procedure for details.)	Frequent perineal care promotes overall hygiene and self esteem.
b. *Encourage* exploration of available incontinence products, such as pads, panties, etc.	Many incontinence products exist. Sampling products aids resident in finding the most satisfactory and comfortable product for that resident.
6. *Teach* Kegel exercises to the resident to strengthen the pelvic floor muscles. Use the following steps:	Use of the Kegel exercises may decrease incontinence if any degree of stress incontinence exists. Stress incontinence is very common, especially in older women.
a. *Instruct* the older woman to stop the flow of urine and then restart it each time she voids. This helps the resident identify the appropriate muscles to contract and relax.	
b. Once the resident is comfortable with locating these muscles while using the toilet, *encourage* her to contract these same muscles while not using the toilet. *Instruct* the resident to contract the muscles and hold the contraction for a few seconds before releasing it. These exercises should be done in a series of ten contractions, several times each day. If the resident is performing these correctly, there should be no observable movement.	
7. *Teach* resident about the importance of adequate hydration and a fiber-filled diet.	Eight to ten glasses of noncaffeinated, nonalcoholic beverages maintain hydration, help to prevent urinary tract infections, and promote bowel motility. A fiber-filled diet also promotes bowel motility.

DOCUMENTATION

1. Collaboration with physician and outcomes of that collaboration, for example, urine specimen obtained, fecal impaction removed, urology consult obtained, medication adjustments made
2. Use of wet/dry checklist, interventions initiated, and results obtained from use of the checklist
3. Presence of any environmental obstacles and interventions initiated to decrease these obstacles
4. Perineal care provided
5. Incontinence products explored and used

6. Resident's attitude toward and success in learning the Kegel exercises and the exercises' impact on incontinence
7. Resident's response toward fluid and fiber intake education
8. Signature and title of nursing staff member

EVALUATION

1. The reasons for the resident's incontinence will be identified.
2. The resident's regular urination pattern will be maintained as closely as possible.
3. The resident's overall hygiene and self esteem will be maintained.
4. The resident will be actively involved in ADL completion.

Nursing System

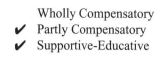

	Wholly Compensatory
✔	Partly Compensatory
✔	Supportive-Educative

OSTOMY CARE
Changing a Colostomy or Ileostomy Appliance

OBJECTIVES

1. To prevent skin excoriation due to irritating fecal material
2. To allow examination of stoma and surrounding skin
3. To encourage the resident's active involvement in completion of ADL

LEVEL OF RESPONSIBILITY

Registered nurse, licensed practical nurse

POLICY

Appliance should be changed daily, usually early in the morning, before breakfast, or before bedtime when there is less bowel activity, and as often as needed between daily changes.

EQUIPMENT

1. Disposable ostomy bag of proper size to fit over the stoma
2. Karaya or other ostomy seal
3. Washcloth and towel
4. Plastic bag for soiled equipment
5. Nonsterile gloves
6. Safety pin

PROCEDURE	RATIONALE
1. *Encourage* resident to *choose* the time for ostomy care.	The ability to choose promotes independence for the resident.
2. At agreed upon time, *explain* procedure to the resident and bring equipment to bedside if resident is bedbound. Assist resident to bathroom if the individual is ambulatory.	
3. Wash your hands.	Hand washing prevents the spread of infection.
4. Put on gloves if assisting with any portion of the ostomy care procedure.	Use of gloves protects both the resident and the nurse and prevents the spread of infection.

PROCEDURE	RATIONALE
5. *Encourage* resident to do as much for self as possible. This could be any or all parts of the ostomy care activity, from removing the used appliance to the entire replacement and cleansing procedure.	Self performance of ostomy care promotes independence and encourages exercise and range of motion.
6. If the resident is bedbound, *assist* to a supine position (see Appendix B) and drape to expose only the stoma. If the resident is ambulatory, *encourage* to assume a comfortable position either standing or sitting.	
7. *Encourage* resident to ask questions during the procedure. *Offer support* and *encouragement* with each step of the procedure performed by the resident.	Ostomy care may represent a significant alteration in self-image. Reinforcement of the resident's progress toward independent self care is essential.
8. Remove soiled ostomy bag and discard in plastic bag.	
9. Cleanse stoma and surrounding skin with warm water and soap. Observe skin and stoma for indications of redness, irritation, or excoriation. *Instruct* resident regarding the importance of these signs and symptoms. If any of these conditions are evident, notify physician. A change in appliance, cleansing method, or adhesive may be indicated.	
10. Apply skin prep to skin surrounding stoma. Allow to air dry.	
11. Apply Karaya adhesive to area surrounding stoma (Figure 5-7). Be sure skin surrounding stoma is clean and dry (Figure 5-8). Center opening of ostomy bag over stoma on top of adhesive (Figures 5-9 and 5-10).	This decreases possibility of skin irritation caused by moisture remaining under bag.
12. Prick top of ostomy bag above opening for stoma with safety pin in two or three places to allow air into and out of the bag. *Reassure* resident that odors will not be a problem if a bag deodorant is used.	If air is not allowed to escape, the bag will gradually inflate and become uncomfortable for the resident under clothing.
13. If ostomy bag with a collar and belt is used, attach belt to collar and secure snugly but comfortably. You should be able to put one hand under the belt comfortably.	

PROCEDURE	**RATIONALE**
14. *Encourage* resident to express feelings at this time regarding the procedure and the individual's performance of the procedure. Continue to *offer encouragement* and praise for the progress made.	Reassurance of the resident's capability for independent self care is essential to reinforce self esteem.
15. *Encourage* and *assist* resident to a comfortable position. If resident is bedbound, place call light within reach.	
16. Dispose of equipment and ostomy bag properly.	
17. Wash your hands.	Hand washing prevents the spread of infection.

Figure 5-7 Karaya Adhesive Applied Around Stoma.

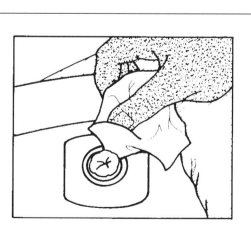

Figure 5-8 Cleanse and Dry Skin Surrounding Stoma.

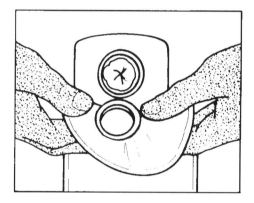

Figure 5-9 Centering Ostomy Bag Opening Over Stoma.

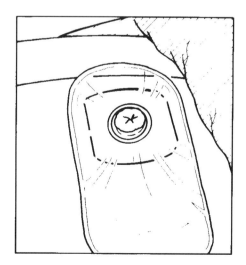

Figure 5-10 Ostomy Bag in Place Over Adhesive.

DOCUMENTATION

1. Date and time of procedure
2. Amount of feces returned, color, consistency, odor, presence of blood or pus
3. Resident's level of participation in the procedure
4. Any concerns expressed by the resident regarding the procedure and/or the individual's participation in the activity
5. Condition of the stoma and surrounding skin, documenting skin color, redness, and any excoriation noted
6. Signature and title of nursing staff member

EVALUATION

1. Resident will understand the procedure for replacement of the ostomy appliance.
2. Resident will be able to express any concerns regarding the use, application, or maintenance of the ostomy appliance.
3. Resident's skin will show no signs of breakdown at the stoma site.
4. Resident will be able to contribute to the self-care process.

Nursing System

Nursing System
Wholly Compensatory
✔ Partly Compensatory
✔ Supportive-Educative

OSTOMY IRRIGATION—COLOSTOMY AND ILEOSTOMY

OBJECTIVES

1. To empty and cleanse the colon
2. To establish a regular pattern of evacuation
3. To encourage resident's active involvement in completion of ADL

LEVEL OF RESPONSIBILITY

Registered nurse, licensed practical nurse

POLICY

Irrigation should be performed at the same time each day, preferably following a meal.

EQUIPMENT

1. Solution as ordered by physician
2. Ostomy irrigation set
3. Lubricant
4. Dressings, if needed
5. Nonsterile gloves
6. Drainage bag and bedpan
7. Plastic bag and plastic protector
8. Washcloth, towel, and soap
9. Waste receptacle

PROCEDURE	RATIONALE
1. *Encourage* resident to *choose* the time for colostomy/ileostomy irrigation.	The ability to choose promotes independence for the resident.
2. At agreed upon time, *explain* procedure to resident and bring equipment to bedside if resident is nonambulatory. If resident is ambulatory, *assist* to attain a comfortable position in the bathroom.	
3. Wash your hands.	Hand washing prevents the spread of infection.
4. Put on gloves if assisting with any portion of the irrigation procedure.	Use of gloves protects both the resident and the nurse and prevents the spread of infection.

PROCEDURE	RATIONALE
5. *Encourage* the resident to do as much of the procedure as possible. This could be any or all parts of the irrigation activity, from removing any dressings and ostomy bag to the entire irrigation procedure.	Self performance of ostomy irrigation promotes independence, self-esteem, and encourages exercise and range of motion.
6. After dressings and bag are removed, cleanse stoma and surrounding skin area with tepid water and mild soap.	
7. Place plastic protector under resident if the individual is bedbound.	
8. Apply drainage bag or irrigation sleeve to ostomy site and place opposite end into bedpan or toilet.	
9. Fill irrigation container with prescribed solution—usually 500 to 1,000 cubic centimeters. Temperature must be tepid (105 to 110 degrees Fahrenheit or 40.5 to 43 degrees Celsius).	Water that is too cold may cause abdominal cramping.
10. Lubricate tip of catheter and expel air by opening clamp until solution flows through tip.	Lubricant eases insertion. Releasing air from tubing prevents abdominal cramping.
11. Insert lubricated tip gently into stoma. Do not insert more than 3 inches (Figure 5-11).	This avoids irritation or possible perforation of the bowel.
12. If resident complains of pain, or resistance is encountered, rotate catheter gently while allowing slow, steady flow of solution.	Allowing solution to flow slowly into stoma will relax the bowel to ease insertion of catheter.
13. If pain or discomfort persists, discontinue procedure and notify charge nurse or physician.	Continuing to insert tip may cause trauma or perforation of the bowel.
14. Open clamp and allow approximately 250 cubic centimeters of solution to flow slowly into the colon. Total volume of solution should be delivered over a 5 to 10 minute period.	Instilling solution too quickly may cause cramping.
15. Leave sleeve in place until return flow is clear—usually within 10 to 15 minutes.	
16. *Encourage* resident to change positions and move about during the 15 minutes following irrigation.	Activity stimulates peristalsis.

PROCEDURE	RATIONALE
17. Remove drainage bag or irrigation sleeve.	
18. Clean and dry stoma and surrounding skin. Apply dressings or ostomy bag as directed in procedure for ostomy care.	
19. *Encourage* resident to *discuss* any feelings regarding the procedure and participation in the self-care activity. *Offer encouragement* regarding the resident's ability to perform the procedure.	Ostomy care can represent a significant alteration in body image. Verbalization of concerns will help counter anxious feelings the resident may be experiencing.
20. If bedbound, leave resident in comfortable position with call light within reach.	
21. Clean and return all equipment to proper place. Discard all disposable equipment properly.	
22. Wash your hands.	Hand washing prevents the spread of infection.

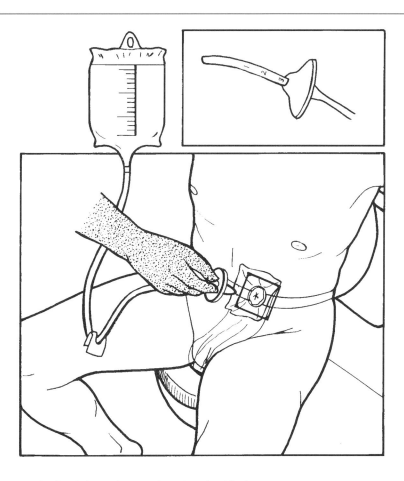

Figure 5-11 Ostomy Irrigation Catheter Tip Inserted No More than 3 Inches.

DOCUMENTATION

1. Time and date of irrigation
2. Amount and type of solution used
3. Condition of the stoma and surrounding area, documenting any irritation or excoriation
4. Amount, color, and consistency of irrigation return
5. Resident's level of participation in the procedure
6. Resident's feelings regarding the procedure and participation in activity
7. Signature and title of nursing staff member

EVALUATION

1. Resident will understand the need for ostomy irrigation.
2. Resident will be able to participate in self care related to ostomy irrigation.
3. Resident will be able to verbalize feelings regarding self care of the ostomy.
4. Resident will be able to recognize signs of irritation and potential problems that may occur while caring for the ostomy site.

Wholly Compensatory
Partly Compensatory
✔ Supportive-Educative

INTAKE AND OUTPUT

OBJECTIVES

1. To maintain an accurate record of the resident's fluid balance
2. To encourage resident's active involvement in self care

LEVEL OF RESPONSIBILITY

Registered nurse, licensed practical nurse, certified nursing assistant

POLICY

Amount and type of fluids given will be as ordered by physician. Data should be recorded every 8 hours and totaled every 24 hours.

EQUIPMENT

1. Intake/output record as designated at facility
2. Bedpan and/or urinal
3. Graduated container
4. Liquid measure chart

PROCEDURE	RATIONALE
1. *Explain* procedure and purpose to resident. Bring equipment to bedside or set up in bathroom.	
2. Wash your hands.	Hand washing prevents the spread of infection.
3. *Ask* resident what location in the room will be most convenient for placing the intake/output record.	This promotes independence, self esteem, and acknowledges respect for the resident's possessions and privacy.
4. *Explain* the amount of fluids and what type of fluids the physician has recommended for the resident.	
5. *Encourage* the resident to do as much for self as possible. This could be any or all parts of the record keeping activity, from selection of fluids to documentation of intake/output.	Self performance of activities promotes independence and self esteem.

PROCEDURE	RATIONALE
6. Measure urine output in urinal or from graduated container if bedpan has been used for elimination.	
7. *Discuss* with the resident the need to maintain adequate fluid balance.	
8. *Assist* if needed with the selection of appropriate fluids.	

DOCUMENTATION

1. Date, amount, and type of fluid selected by resident recorded every 8 hours
2. Total of intake and output every 24 hours
3. Resident's skin turgor, condition of mucous membranes, presence of edema, presence of lung congestion
4. Amount of self care resident was able to perform
5. Signature and title of nursing staff member

EVALUATION

1. The resident will understand the need to maintain adequate fluid balance each day.
2. The resident will be able to select the types of fluid used each day.
3. The resident will display no signs of dehydration or fluid overload.
4. The resident will be able to participate in the record keeping process.

chapter 6

Instrumental Activities of Daily Living

Nursing System

✔	Wholly Compensatory
	Partly Compensatory
	Supportive-Educative

BED MAKING—OCCUPIED

OBJECTIVES

1. To provide a clean, comfortable environment for the resident
2. To encourage resident's active involvement in completion of IADL

LEVEL OF RESPONSIBILITY

Registered nurse, licensed practical nurse, certified nursing assistant

POLICY

Bed linen should be changed daily and as needed if resident is bedbound and/or incontinent. While changing an occupied bed, the resident's skin should be examined for indications of breakdown or redness. At this time also, a back rub can be given if resident has been bedbound or if the resident requests the nurse to do so.

EQUIPMENT

1. Sheets and pillowcase
2. Drawsheet
3. Bedspread

4. Blanket
5. Dirty linen hamper
6. Rolled bath towel

PROCEDURE	RATIONALE
1. *Encourage* resident to *choose* the time for bed making.	The ability to choose promotes independence for the resident.
2. At agreed upon time, *explain* procedure to the resident and bring equipment to the bedside.	
3. Screen the resident for privacy.	
4. Wash your hands.	Hand washing prevents the spread of infection.
5. Raise the bed to waist height.	This minimizes the possibility of back strain for the nurse.
6. *Encourage* resident to *assist* with bed making as much as possible. This could be as little as holding a side rail to maintain a position or adjusting legs or arms to facilitate the activity.	Self performance of the task at any level of participation promotes independence and encourages exercise and range of motion.
7. Loosen top bedding at the foot of the bed. Remove blanket and bedspread. Fold and place on chair.	
8. Raise side rail. Go to other side of bed. If resident is able, *encourage* to turn to the side with rail up, back facing you. *Ask* resident to hold on to side rail if possible. *Assist* to maintain position if needed.	
9. Loosen sheet from under mattress. Fold toward resident's back.	
10. Place folded, clean, large sheet on bed. Roll it toward resident. Tuck sheet under the mattress at the head of the bed.	
11. Place the drawsheet, folding it toward the middle of the bed. Use plastic drawsheet only if the resident is incontinent.	
12. *Encourage* and *assist* resident to turn toward you and roll over the linen that is gathered to the middle of the bed. Raise the side rail nearest you. *Ask* resident to hold on to the side rail as before.	

PROCEDURE	RATIONALE
13. Go to the other side of the bed and take soiled linen off bed. Dispose of properly in linen hamper. Tuck clean sheets under mattress and miter corners. Pull drawsheet tightly and tuck under the mattress.	
14. *Encourage* and *assist* resident to assume a supine position. Place clean top sheet over resident. Hold hem of clean sheet and draw soiled sheet out toward foot of the bed.	
15. Do not expose the resident.	This maintains privacy for the resident and avoids unnecessary chilling.
16. Place blanket and spread on bed. Allow sufficient room for resident to move feet freely.	Pressure on the toes can lead to skin breakdown on toes or heels.
17. Change pillowcase. Provide support for resident's neck during change with a rolled bath towel.	
18. Adjust height of the bed to lowest position or according to resident's preference if appropriate.	
19. Place call light within reach of the resident and pull side rails up.	
20. Wash your hands.	Hand washing prevents the spread of infection.

DOCUMENTATION

1. Date and time bed was changed
2. Resident's participation in the activity and reaction
3. Condition of the resident's skin, and if a back rub was given, resident's reaction
4. Signature and title of nursing staff

EVALUATION

1. Resident's bed linen will be clean and dry each day.
2. Resident will be able to assist with the activity to some degree, depending on condition.
3. Resident's skin will be free of irritation caused by soiled linen or wrinkled linen.
4. If back rub was given, resident will be relaxed and comforted by the activity.

Nursing System

Wholly Compensatory
✔ Partly Compensatory
✔ Supportive-Educative

BED MAKING—UNOCCUPIED

OBJECTIVES

1. To provide a clean, comfortable environment for the resident
2. To encourage resident's active involvement in completion of IADL

LEVEL OF RESPONSIBILITY

Registered nurse, licensed practical nurse, certified nursing assistant

POLICY

Bed linen should be changed twice a week if resident is ambulatory during the day and continent. Change linen daily and whenever needed if resident is incontinent.

EQUIPMENT

1. Sheets and pillowcase
2. Drawsheet
3. Blanket
4. Bedspread
5. Plastic protector, if needed
6. Dirty linen hamper

PROCEDURE	RATIONALE
1. *Encourage* resident to *choose* the time for linen change.	The ability to choose promotes independence for the resident.
2. At agreed upon time, take linen to bedside and place on chair in the order to be used.	
3. *Encourage* resident to perform as much of the task as possible. This could be any or all aspects of the activity, from removing soiled linen to completion of the entire project with or without nursing staff supervision.	Self performance of the bed making activity promotes independence and encourages exercise and range of motion.

PROCEDURE	RATIONALE
4. Adjust bed to a flat position. Elevate bed to waist height.	This minimizes possible back strain for resident or staff member.
5. Loosen linen and roll to the head of the bed. Bundle soiled linen into bottom sheet.	
6. Dispose of dirty linen in linen hamper.	
7. Place the bottom sheet evenly at the foot of the mattress with the center fold at the center of the bed (Figure 6-1). Open sheet as shown in Figure 6-2.	
8. Tuck the sheet under the head of the mattress (Figure 6-3). Miter the corners and tuck the sides under the mattress as shown in Figures 6-4 and 6-5.	
9. Place drawsheet in the center of the bed (Figure 6-6). Place plastic protector under drawsheet if resident is incontinent.	
10. Tuck in drawsheet.	
11. Place the top sheet so that the hem is even with the head of the mattress. Cover sheet with the blanket approximately 8 inches from the top of the sheet.	
12. Place top edge of the bedspread even with the mattress.	
13. Tuck the bedding at the foot of the bed. Miter the corners.	
14. If the bed is to be occupied immediately, fan fold top bedding to the foot of the bed.	
15. Place pillowcase on pillow.	
16. Adjust the position of the bed for resident comfort and preference. Adjust the height of the bed to the lowest position.	
17. Any of the above steps should be *adjusted to meet* the *personal preference* of the resident.	
18. Wash your hands.	Hand washing prevents the spread of infection.

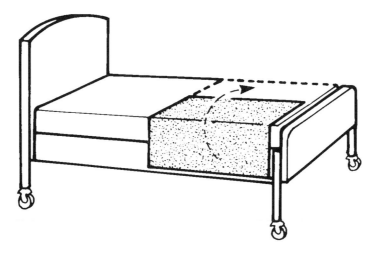

Figure 6-1 Bottom Sheet Placed at Foot of Bed with Center Fold at Center of Bed.

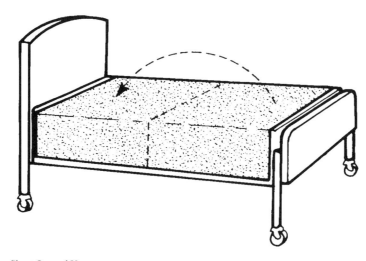

Figure 6-2 Bottom Sheet Opened Up.

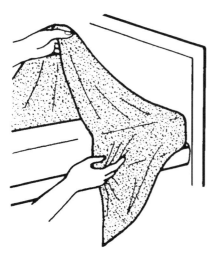

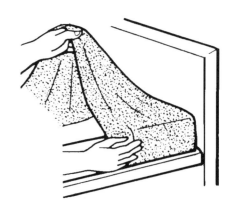

Figure 6-3 Sheet Tucked Under Head of Mattress.   **Figure 6-4** Mitering Corner.

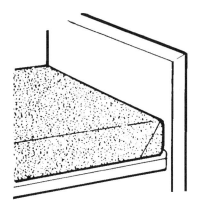

Figure 6-5 Sides of Sheet Tucked Under Mattress.

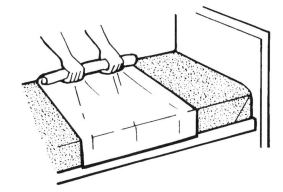

Figure 6-6 Drawsheet Placed in Center of Bed.

DOCUMENTATION

1. Date and time bed was made
2. Resident's involvement in the activity
3. Signature and title of nursing staff member

EVALUATION

1. Resident will have a clean, dry bed.
2. Resident will participate in the bed making project.

Nursing System

Wholly Compensatory
Partly Compensatory
✔ Supportive-Educative

MEDICATION—EAR

OBJECTIVES

1. To treat an infection of the auditory canal
2. To relieve inflammation and pain
3. To encourage the resident's active involvement in self care

LEVEL OF RESPONSIBILITY

Registered nurse, licensed practical nurse

POLICY

Ear drops are administered only with a physician's order and only to the ear requiring treatment.

EQUIPMENT

1. Medication as prescribed
2. Gauze squares (4 by 4 inches) or cotton balls
3. Small basin of warm water
4. Nonsterile gloves

PROCEDURE	RATIONALE
1. If compatible with physician's orders, *encourage* the resident to *choose* the time for ear drop procedure.	The ability to choose promotes independence for the resident.
2. At agreed upon time, *explain* the purpose and procedure to the resident.	
3. Gather equipment and bring to bedside.	
4. Wash your hands.	Hand washing prevents the spread of infection.
5. If nursing staff member is performing the procedure, put on gloves.	Use of gloves protects both the resident and the nurse and prevents the spread of infection.
6. *Encourage* resident to do as much self care as possible. This may include any portion of the procedure, from warming the medication to instillation of the medication.	Self performance of medication administration promotes independence for the resident.

PROCEDURE	**RATIONALE**
7. Instillation may be accomplished with resident sitting in a chair with head tilted away from the affected ear or lying on the unaffected side with the affected ear in an upward position toward the ceiling.	
8. Place medication container in a small basin of warm water to achieve room temperature. Test a drop of medication on wrist for correct temperature.	This will be the most comfortable temperature for the affected ear and for the resident's tolerance of the application.
9. Straighten the auditory canal by holding the auricle upward and backward (Figure 6-7).	The adult auditory canal is long and composed mostly of bone. This angle promotes straightening of the adult auditory canal.
10. If nurse is assisting, instill medication with hand resting on resident's cheek for stabilization, in the amount ordered by the physician. If resident is instilling medication, brace applicator tip against outer ear canal.	
11. Insert small cotton ball in the external auditory canal to contain medication.	
12. *Instruct* resident to remain in this position with affected ear upward for 10 to 15 minutes.	This allows medication to penetrate inflamed tissues.
13. Clean equipment. Discard disposable items properly.	
14. Return ear drops to appropriate storage area.	
15. Wash your hands.	Hand washing prevents the spread of infection.
16. Allow resident time to *discuss* any concerns or questions about the procedure and the purpose.	
17. After 10 to 15 minutes, resident may sit upright if desired. Leave resident in a comfortable position.	

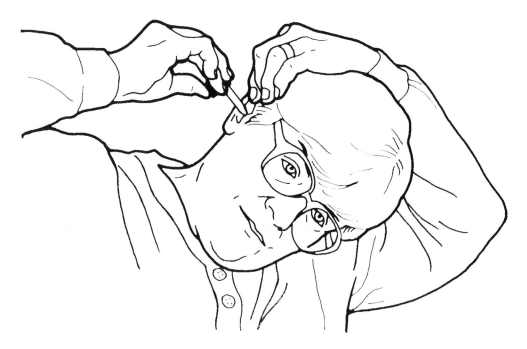

Figure 6-7 Auditory Canal Straightened by Holding the Auricle Upward and Backward.

DOCUMENTATION

1. Date and time medication was administered
2. Type of medication and amount instilled
3. Which ear was medicated
4. Type, color, and amount of cerumen and/or drainage from ear
5. Resident's participation and understanding of the procedure
6. Signature and title of nursing staff member

EVALUATION

1. The auditory canal will be free from infection and irritation.
2. The resident will participate in self administration of medication.
3. The resident will understand the purpose of the procedure.

	Wholly Compensatory
	Partly Compensatory
✔	Supportive-Educative

MEDICATION—EYE

OBJECTIVES

1. To treat an eye infection
2. To relieve inflammation and pain
3. To dilate or contract the pupil for specific medical conditions
4. To encourage the resident's active involvement in self care

LEVEL OF RESPONSIBILITY

Registered nurse, licensed practical nurse

POLICY

Eye drops are administered only with a physician's order and only to the eye or eyes requiring treatment.

EQUIPMENT

1. Medication as prescribed
2. Gauze square (4 by 4 inches) or cotton balls
3. Nonsterile gloves

PROCEDURE	RATIONALE
1. If compatible with physician's orders, *encourage* the resident to *choose* the time and place for the procedure.	The ability to choose promotes independence for the resident.
2. At agreed upon time, *explain* the purpose and procedure to the resident.	
3. Gather equipment and bring to agreed upon location. Installation can be accomplished in bed with resident in a supine position (see Appendix B) or sitting in a chair with the head tilted back.	
4. Wash your hands.	Hand washing prevents the spread of infection.
5. If nursing staff member is assisting with any portion of the procedure, put on gloves.	Use of gloves protects both the resident and the nurse and prevents the spread of infection.

PROCEDURE	**RATIONALE**
6. *Encourage* resident to do as much of the procedure as possible.	Self performance of medication administration promotes independence for the resident.
7. Stand behind resident if administration is performed by nursing staff.	This allows closer examination of the eye and easier access to administer medication.
8. Using a cotton ball, wipe any accumulated secretions from inner canthus to outer edge. Use a different cotton ball for each eye.	Risk of infection or reinfection caused by secretions is decreased by wiping outward. Using a different cotton ball for each eye ensures that infection will not be spread from one eye to the other.
9. Draw prescribed amount of medication into dropper if liquid medication is used. Check physician's order regarding eye or eyes requiring medication.	To prevent contamination, never draw more than the prescribed amount. Avoid pushing remainder back into bottle. Prevent medication error by always verifying the eye being treated.
10. *Encourage* and *assist* resident to tilt head backward. Gently pull lower lid down. Ask resident to look upward at the ceiling (see Figure 6-8).	This exposes the eye area as much as possible and prevents medication from dripping on the cornea.
11. Support hand on resident's forehead or bridge of nose. If resident is performing the procedure, *instruct* to do the same.	This prevents dropper tip from touching eye or lids and avoids possible eye injury should resident move suddenly.
12. Introduce drop to center of lower lid. If ointment is used, apply as a thin strip of medication to lower lid.	
13. *Instruct* resident to close eyes slowly and gently, not to squeeze eyes shut.	Forcing eyes shut will push medication out of the eye. Gentle closing allows the medication to be distributed over the entire eye surface.
14. Wipe off any excess medication with a clean cotton ball or gauze square.	
15. Dispose of gloves and used cotton balls or gauze properly.	
16. Return eye drops or ointment to appropriate storage area.	
17. Wash your hands.	Hand washing prevents the spread of infection.
18. Allow resident time to *discuss* any concerns or questions about the procedure and purpose.	

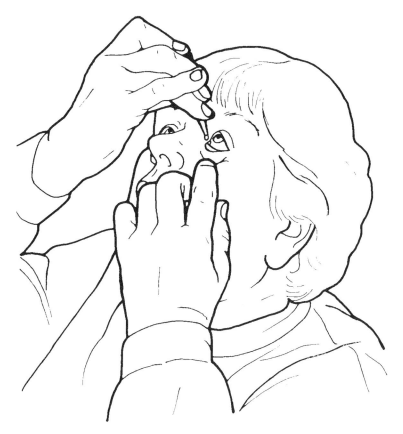

Figure 6-8 Positioning for Administration of Eye Medication.

DOCUMENTATION

1. Date and time of medication administration
2. Type and amount of medication given (drops or ointment)
3. Which eye was medicated
4. Condition of the eye, noting color and amount of drainage
5. Resident's participation and understanding of the procedure
6. Signature and title of nursing staff member

EVALUATION

1. The eye or eyes will be free from infection and irritation.
2. The resident will participate in self administration of medication.
3. The resident will understand the purpose for the procedure.

MEDICATION—NOSE DROPS

OBJECTIVES

1. To promote a clear nasal airway
2. To encourage resident's active involvement in completion of IADL

LEVEL OF RESPONSIBILITY

Registered nurse, licensed practical nurse

EQUIPMENT

1. Nose drops with medication dropper as prescribed by physician

PROCEDURE	RATIONALE
1. Wash your hands.	Hand washing prevents the spread of infection.
2. *Teach* the resident the following key concepts of medication administration.	Education regarding procedures promotes independence for the resident through increasing knowledge and acquisition of a new skill.
a. Read medication label and note the name of medication, name of resident, and dosage.	
b. Note time of medication administration on resident's own medication administration card.	
3. *Encourage* resident to utilize the following steps for nose drop administration. If teaching this skill to the resident, *demonstrate* the procedure and *encourage* the resident to practice with you. Repeat teaching sessions until both you and the resident feel confident about the resident's ability to perform this new skill.	New skill acquisition often requires frequent teaching sessions with return demonstrations. Positive reinforcement will encourage the resident to continue to practice the new skill.
a. Assume a sitting position with head tilted backward.	

PROCEDURE	RATIONALE
b. Using the nondominant hand, gently push the nasal septum upward as in Figure 6-9.	In this position, the nasal opening is angled for easy drop administration.
c. Using the dominant hand, instill drops as prescribed.	
d. Maintain the head in the tilted backward position for a minute and gently inhale.	Holding this position encourages distribution of nose drops.
4. Wash your hands.	Hand washing prevents the spread of infection.
5. *Encourage* resident to maintain her/his own medication record and to document this administration.	Maintaining a medication record will encourage appropriate administration and offer health care professionals an opportunity to observe resident's own medication management.

Figure 6-9 Positioning for Administration of Nose Drops.

DOCUMENTATION

1. Name and dosage of medication
2. Date and time medication was taken
3. Resident's ability to self administer nose drops
4. Signature and title of nursing staff member

EVALUATION

1. The resident will breathe freely and have a clear nasal airway.
2. The resident will be actively involved in completion of IADL.

Nursing System

Wholly Compensatory
✔ Partly Compensatory
✔ Supportive-Educative

MEDICATION—ORAL AND SUBLINGUAL

OBJECTIVES

1. To administer medication in the proper dose, by the appropriate route, and at the specified time
2. To treat injury and disease
3. To encourage the resident's active involvement in self care

LEVEL OF RESPONSIBILITY

Registered nurse, licensed practical nurse with pharmacology training

POLICY

Medication is given only with a physician's order at the time ordered and by the route ordered.

EQUIPMENT

1. Medication
2. Medicine cup
3. Stethoscope
4. Watch with second hand
5. Water or juice

PROCEDURE	RATIONALE
1. Gather equipment. Check physician's order against the medication available.	Guard against any discrepancy in the medication order versus the medication available for the resident.
2. Bring medication to the resident's room or ask resident to come to a convenient location for administration.	The ability to choose promotes independence for the resident.
3. Know each medication's action and side effects before administering. *Encourage* the resident to be aware of the same and to *report* any reactions immediately to the nursing staff.	This promotes independence and increases self esteem for the resident.
4. Wash your hands.	Hand washing prevents the spread of infection.

PROCEDURE	RATIONALE
5. *Ask* if the resident prefers medication to be given one at a time or all at once. *Encourage* resident to identify each medication, how often it is taken, and its purpose.	This encourages independence and self esteem for the resident and reinforces the importance of each medication.
6. Follow appropriate steps below for cardiac, liquid, and/or tablet medications. Other routes and types of medications, such as intravenous, intramuscular, and subcutaneous are not discussed since they relate to a level of care not addressed in this book.	

Cardiac Medications

1. Take blood pressure and check apical pulse using a stethoscope and watch or clock with a second hand for a full minute before administering any cardiac medication. Resident can be *instructed* to check apical pulse by placing hand over heart and using a watch with a second hand. *Review* technique with resident until accurate measurement can be determined by resident.	Unless otherwise indicated by the physician, cardiac medications are usually given only when blood pressure and apical pulse are within a specified range.

Liquid Medications

1. Shake medication before pouring into medicine cup.	
2. Pour medication away from label.	This avoids obscuring label instructions.
3. Hold medicine cup with liquid at eye level.	This allows more accurate measurement of dosage.
4. Do not offer water or juice after administering liquid medication unless ordered by physician.	Some liquids are meant to coat the throat. Water will dilute the desired effect.
5. When giving oil-based medications, offer juice or water after administering.	Water or fruit juice will not alter the therapeutic effect of the medication and will make it more palatable.
6. *Review* above techniques and rationales with resident until resident is comfortable with them.	

Tablet Medications

1. Check the *Physician's Desk Reference* before administering or altering tablets.	Some tablets may be crushed if necessary for the resident to swallow. Enteric coated tablets cannot be crushed since absorption takes place in the gastrointestinal tract, not in the stomach.

PROCEDURE	RATIONALE
	Others, such as some antibiotics, cannot be given with certain liquids that will affect the composition of the medication. Sublingual tablets are only placed under the tongue and are not followed by any liquids since dilution of the medication is not desired.
2. *Review* with the resident the above rationale for offering different medications in differing ways.	This promotes understanding and decreases knowledge deficits that may lead to medication errors by the resident.
3. If a tablet is accidentally dropped on the floor, discard it and give another.	The floor is considered highly contaminated.
4. Remain with the resident until all of the medication is swallowed.	This increases safety in case of any swallowing difficulty and allows the nurse to record accurately that the medication has been administered. If the nurse has not seen the resident swallow the medication, it cannot be recorded that it was administered.
5. Return unused medication to the appropriate storage area. Discard disposable items.	
6. Wash your hands.	Hand washing prevents the spread of infection.
7. Allow resident time to *discuss* concerns or *ask* questions regarding the medication given or any medical condition.	This promotes knowledge, understanding, and self esteem for the resident.

DOCUMENTATION

1. Date, time, route, and name of each medication given
2. Record of any medication refused or omitted and the reason
3. Record of any adverse reaction to the medication given, date and time of physician notification of reaction
4. Resident's level of participation in administration of the medication
5. Signature and title of nursing staff member

EVALUATION

1. The resident will receive the appropriate medication at the appropriate time, by the appropriate route.
2. The resident's condition for which medication is given will improve.
3. The resident will have increased knowledge regarding the medication given and the need for each medication given.
4. The resident will increase the level of participation in self care.

MEDICATION—RECTAL SUPPOSITORIES

OBJECTIVES

1. To provide relief for acute episode of constipation
2. To encourage the resident's active involvement in completion of IADL

LEVEL OF RESPONSIBILITY

Registered nurse, licensed practical nurse

EQUIPMENT

1. Suppository as prescribed by the physician
2. Disposable glove
3. Water soluble lubricant
4. Disposable tissues

PROCEDURE	RATIONALE
1. Wash your hands.	Hand washing prevents the spread of infection.
2. *Teach* the resident the following key concepts of medication administration:	Education regarding procedures promotes independence for the resident through increasing knowledge and acquisition of a new skill.
a. Read medication label and note name of medication, name of resident, and dosage.	
b. Note time of medication on resident's own medication administration card.	
3. *Encourage* resident to utilize the following steps for suppository insertion:	
a. Lie on side with knees bent.	This position promotes easier suppository insertion.
b. Put glove on dominant hand.	
c. Lubricate tip of suppository and index finger.	

PROCEDURE	RATIONALE
d. Insert suppository into rectum with index finger (approximately 1 ½ inches).	
e. Wipe anal area with disposable tissues.	
f. Remove glove and discard.	
4. Wash your hands.	Hand washing prevents the spread of infection.
5. *Encourage* resident to maintain her/his own medication record and to document this administration.	Maintaining a medication record will encourage appropriate administration and offer health care professionals an opportunity to observe the resident's own medication management.

DOCUMENTATION

1. Name and dose of medication
2. Date and time medication was taken
3. Resident's ability to self administer suppository
4. Signature and title of nursing staff member

EVALUATION

1. The resident will be free of constipation and will maintain her/his normal pattern of defecation.
2. The resident will be actively involved in completion of IADL.

chapter 7

Health Assessment and Special Skills

Nursing System

✔	Wholly Compensatory
	Partly Compensatory
✔	Supportive-Educative

BACK RUB

OBJECTIVES

1. To promote comfort and relaxation through therapeutic use of touch
2. To increase circulation to underlying musculature
3. To encourage resident's active involvement in completion of treatments

LEVEL OF RESPONSIBILITY

Registered nurse, licensed practical nurse, certified nursing assistant

EQUIPMENT

1. Lotion
2. Soft blanket or sheet

PROCEDURE	RATIONALE
1. *Encourage* resident to *choose* time for a back rub.	The ability to choose promotes independence for the resident.

PROCEDURE	RATIONALE
2. At agreed upon time, *explain* procedure to resident and bring equipment to bedside.	
3. Wash your hands.	Hand washing prevents the spread of infection.
4. Prepare the environment/room.	
a. Keep the room at a comfortable, warm temperature.	A warm, private space prevents the resident from becoming chilled and promotes relaxation.
b. Keep the door closed.	
c. If resident desires, have a radio set to soft, quiet music.	Soft music also aids relaxation.
5. *Encourage* resident to lie in prone position. If unable to lie in prone position, *encourage* resident to assume side lying position.	
6. Adjust height of bed in comfortable position for you.	Comfortable bed height helps prevent back strain for nursing staff member.
7. Keep resident covered with sheet or blanket, exposing only back area.	Use of sheet promotes privacy and warmth.
8. Pour generous amount of lotion in palm of your hand. Rub your hands together.	Rubbing your hands together warms your hands and the lotion.
9. Begin the massage using the following steps:	
a. Position one hand on each side of the spine at the level of the lower back.	
b. Using the heel of the thumb and a constant, firm yet comfortable pressure, move up the spine creating small, circular motions.	
c. At the shoulder muscles, use a kneading type of stroke.	
d. At the end of the massage, use larger and softer circles up and down back area.	
10. After the massage, *encourage* and *assist* resident to attain a comfortable position.	
11. Discard used linen appropriately.	
12. Wash your hands.	Hand washing prevents the spread of infection.

DOCUMENTATION

1. Date and time back rub was given
2. Ability of resident to turn and position self and participate in treatment
3. Presence of any reddened or discolored skin areas, dry or irritated skin, or any other unusual findings
4. Signature and title of nursing staff member

EVALUATION

1. The resident will be relaxed and calm.
2. The resident will be actively involved in completion of treatments.

Nursing System

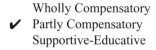

Wholly Compensatory
✔ Partly Compensatory
Supportive-Educative

CALL LIGHT SYSTEM/VERBAL RESPONSES

OBJECTIVES

1. To provide the resident access to assistance or support from staff at all times
2. To encourage feelings of security and trust between resident and staff

LEVEL OF RESPONSIBILITY

Registered nurse, licensed practical nurse, certified nursing assistant

PROCEDURE	RATIONALE
1. Staff is visible to residents at all times.	Staff visibility promotes security and trust between resident and staff.
2. For those residents who are less mobile and are unable to independently ambulate in order to make a request of staff, the call light is important. The following considerations are to be kept in mind:	
a. Keep call light within easy reach of the resident.	
b. *Answer* call light promptly.	The resident may have an urgent need.
c. Be courteous and calm when entering room. *Ask* the resident, "How may I be of help?"	
d. *Listen* to the resident's request.	
e. *Respond* to the resident's request.	
3. Verbal interaction between resident and staff is important for all residents. The following considerations are to be kept in mind during all interactions:	
a. Be courteous and calm.	
b. Be *supportive* and *encouraging*.	
c. Be familiar with the resident's abilities and *encourage* independent activity.	

EVALUATION

1. The resident will be able to access assistance or support from staff at all times.
2. The resident will trust and feel secure in her/his home environment.

Nursing System

	Wholly Compensatory
✔	Partly Compensatory
✔	Supportive-Educative

DRESSING CHANGE—NONSTERILE

OBJECTIVES

1. To promote comfort, support, immobilization, pressure, or absorption
2. To prevent irritation
3. To prevent bacteria from entering a wound and to prevent the spread of infection from the wound
4. To encourage the resident's active involvement in the completion of treatments

LEVEL OF RESPONSIBILITY

Registered nurse, licensed practical nurse

POLICY

Dressings should be changed as ordered by the physician if application of a medication is indicated. If the dressing is a dry, protective covering, change as needed to maintain cleanliness but remember also the need to reduce irritation caused by disturbing the wound site.

EQUIPMENT

1. Dressings and tape
2. Prescribed cleansing solution
3. Prescribed medication
4. Plastic bag for soiled dressings
5. Adhesive remover
6. Nonsterile gloves

PROCEDURE	RATIONALE
1. *Encourage* resident to *choose* the time for dressing change.	The ability to choose promotes independence for the resident.
2. At agreed upon time, *explain* the procedure and purpose to the resident.	
3. *Encourage* and *assist* resident to attain a comfortable position compatible with the location of the wound to be dressed.	
4. Gather equipment and bring to the resident's room.	

PROCEDURE	RATIONALE
5. Screen for privacy.	
6. Adjust lighting if necessary to facilitate assessment of the wound and the dressing care.	
7. *Encourage* the resident to do as much of the procedure as possible. This could be any or all parts of the dressing change activity.	Self performance of the dressing change promotes independence and encourages exercise and range of motion.
8. Wash your hands.	Hand washing prevents the spread of infection.
9. If the nursing staff is assisting with any portion of the dressing change, put on gloves.	Use of gloves protects both the resident and the nurse and prevents the spread of infection.
10. Remove soiled dressings. Place in plastic bag.	
11. *Examine* the wound for signs of irritation, redness, warmth, or drainage. *Explain* to the resident that these signs, if they occur, may indicate an infection.	This encourages the resident's participation in self care and increases self esteem for the resident.
12. Open dressing pack. If ordered, cleanse area to be dressed with prescribed solution or warm water.	
13. Remove old adhesive with remover, taking care not to get the solution into the wound.	
14. Apply medication if ordered by physician.	
15. Apply dressings and secure with tape. Dressings should cling and conform to body contours. Use as little tape as possible in direct contact with the skin to reduce irritation.	Gaps should be avoided, unless air circulation is required, since gaps allow the accumulation of secretions and may promote growth of bacteria.
16. Discard gloves in plastic bag.	
17. *Assist* resident to a comfortable position.	
18. Return any reusable equipment to an appropriate area.	
19. Discard bag containing dressings and gloves in infectious waste container.	
20. Wash your hands.	Hand washing prevents the spread of infection.

DOCUMENTATION

1. Date and time of dressing change
2. Cleansing solution used
3. Condition of the wound, noting color, drainage, redness, and warmth
4. Resident's level of participation in self care and understanding of signs and symptoms to be reported to nursing staff
5. Signature and title of nursing staff member

EVALUATION

1. The wound will be free of infection and irritation.
2. Resident will be able to participate in the procedure.
3. Resident will have an understanding of adverse signs and symptoms to be reported to the physician or nursing staff member.

Nursing System

✔ Wholly Compensatory
Partly Compensatory
✔ Supportive-Educative

DRESSING CHANGE—STERILE

OBJECTIVES

1. To prevent bacteria from entering a wound and to prevent the spread of infection from the wound
2. To prevent irritation
3. To encourage the resident's active involvement in the completion of treatments

LEVEL OF RESPONSIBILITY

Registered nurse, licensed practical nurse

POLICY

Sterile dressings are changed by order of the physician. In most cases, the resident will probably not be performing a sterile dressing change without assistance from the nursing staff or family member.

EQUIPMENT

1. Sterile dressing package
2. Sterile gloves
3. Nonsterile gloves
4. Prescribed cleansing solution
5. Prescribed medication
6. Plastic bag for soiled dressings
7. Adhesive remover

PROCEDURE	RATIONALE
1. If compatible with physician's orders, *encourage* the resident to *choose* the time for a dressing change.	The ability to choose promotes independence for the resident.
2. At agreed upon time, *explain* the procedure and purpose to the resident.	
3. *Encourage* and *assist* the resident to attain a comfortable position compatible with the location of the wound to be dressed.	
4. Gather equipment and bring to the resident's room.	

PROCEDURE	RATIONALE
5. Screen for privacy.	
6. Adjust the lighting if necessary to facilitate assessment of the wound and the dressing care.	
7. Wash your hands.	Hand washing prevents the spread of infection.
8. *Encourage* the resident to do as much of the nonsterile portion of the procedure as possible.	Self performance of the dressing change promotes independence and encourages exercise and range of motion.
9. Put on nonsterile gloves.	Use of nonsterile gloves protects the nurse and resident from contaminated dressings.
10. Remove soiled dressings. Place in plastic bag.	
11. Remove any adhesive remaining on the skin with the adhesive remover, taking care not to get solution into wound.	
12. *Examine* the wound for signs of irritation, redness, warmth, or drainage. *Explain* to the resident that these signs, if they occur, may indicate an infection.	This encourages the resident's participation in self care and increases self esteem for the resident.
13. Remove nonsterile gloves and discard in plastic bag.	
14. Prepare sterile field by placing sterile drape as near as possible to wound site.	Gaps may allow sterile dressings to come in contact with nonsterile areas.
15. Open sterile dressing package and empty contents onto sterile field, being careful not to touch the contents.	
16. Pour prescribed solution onto gauze to be used for cleaning.	
17. After all necessary packages and containers have been opened, put on sterile gloves.	Sterile gloves are used only when all nonsterile items have been handled to avoid contamination of the wound site or sterile dressing.
18. Apply prescribed medication to the wound.	
19. Apply sterile dressings and secure with tape. Be sure there are no gaps in the dressing.	Gaps allow the accumulation of exudates and promote the growth of bacteria.
20. Remove sterile gloves and discard in plastic bag.	

PROCEDURE	RATIONALE
21. *Assist* resident to attain a comfortable position.	
22. Return any reusable equipment to an appropriate area.	
23. Discard bag containing dressings and gloves in infectious waste container.	
24. Wash your hands.	Hand washing prevents the spread of infection.

DOCUMENTATION

1. Date and time of dressing change
2. Cleansing solution used
3. Condition of the wound, noting color, drainage, redness, and warmth
4. Resident's level of participation in self care and understanding of signs and symptoms to be reported to the nursing staff
5. Signature and title of nursing staff member

EVALUATION

1. The wound will be clean, dry, and free of infection.
2. Sterile technique will be observed.
3. The resident will understand the need to maintain the sterility of the area.
4. The resident will reach a level of participation in the care of the wound.

Nursing System

	Wholly Compensatory
	Partly Compensatory
✔	Supportive-Educative

ASSESSMENT OF PULSE—RADIAL

OBJECTIVES

1. To obtain accurate pulse rate
2. To encourage resident's involvement in and understanding of health assessment skills

LEVEL OF RESPONSIBILITY

Registered nurse, licensed practical nurse

EQUIPMENT

1. Watch with second hand

PROCEDURE	RATIONALE
1. Wash your hands.	Hand washing prevents the spread of infection.
2. *Teach* the resident the following key concepts of pulse assessment:	Education regarding procedures promotes independence for the resident through increasing knowledge and acquisition of a new skill.
a. Reason for pulse assessment.	Pulse rate is a reflection of the heart's functioning and can be influenced by some medications.
b. Type of medications the resident is taking that may influence pulse rate.	
c. Frequency with which pulse rate should be assessed.	Physician may suggest frequency of pulse rate assessment in order to monitor the resident's response to medication or to elicit information regarding the resident's condition.
3. Use the following steps for pulse rate assessment. If teaching this skill to the resident, *demonstrate* the procedure and *encourage* the resident to practice with you. Repeat teaching sessions until both you and the resident feel confident about the resident's ability to perform this new skill.	New skill acquisition often requires frequent teaching sessions with return demonstrations. Positive reinforcement will encourage the resident to continue to practice the new skill.

PROCEDURE	RATIONALE
a. *Encourage* resident to assume a sitting position with one arm resting in lap, elbow bent at a 90 degree angle and palm facing up. If resident is right handed, the left arm should be in her/his lap and vice versa.	
b. Using two or three fingertips, compress the radial artery against the distal radius (see Figure 7-1). Do not use your thumb.	The radial pulse is the most convenient to use and easiest to find on oneself. The thumb has a pulsation of its own and may interfere with evaluation.
c. Using watch with a second hand, count the pulsations for a full minute. Note the pulse's rate and rhythm.	
4. Wash your hands.	Hand washing prevents the spread of infection.

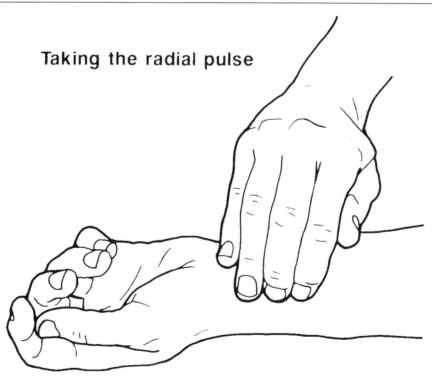

Taking the radial pulse

Figure 7-1 Two or Three Fingertips Are Used To Assess Radial Pulse.

DOCUMENTATION

1. Date and time of pulse assessment
2. Pulse rate and rhythm
3. Resident's ability and skill level of pulse evaluation
4. Signature and title of nursing staff member

EVALUATION

1. The resident will be able to obtain her/his own pulse rate accurately.
2. The resident will express interest in learning about radial pulse assessment.

✔ Wholly Compensatory
✔ Partly Compensatory
✔ Supportive-Educative

SPECIMEN COLLECTION

OBJECTIVE

To obtain a sample of specific body fluids for diagnostic purposes

LEVEL OF RESPONSIBILITY

Registered nurse, licensed practical nurse

POLICY

All specimen collection is performed by order of the physician only.

THROAT SPECIMEN

OBJECTIVE

1. To determine the cause and initiate treatment for complaints of a sore throat

EQUIPMENT

1. Commercially prepared culture tube kit
2. Tongue blade
3. Penlight
4. Nonsterile gloves

PROCEDURE	RATIONALE
1. *Explain* procedure and purpose to the resident.	
2. Put on gloves.	Use of gloves protects both the resident and the nurse and prevents the spread of infection.
3. *Ask* resident to open mouth and extend tongue.	
4. If visualization of the throat and surrounding tissues is impaired, use tongue blade and a penlight.	

PROCEDURE	RATIONALE
5. Swab any reddened areas, white areas, or those with exudates using the swab contained in the culture tube kit.	These areas are probable sites of infection.
6. Immediately place the swab into the culture tube. Follow directions enclosed for crushing ampule and storage of the tube until it can be transported to the laboratory for analysis.	
7. Dispose of gloves properly.	
8. Wash your hands.	Hand washing prevents the spread of infection.
9. Prepare laboratory requisition form according to agency or facility policy.	

DOCUMENTATION

1. Date and time specimen was obtained
2. Appearance of the throat and surrounding tissues where specimen was obtained
3. Appearance of any exudate in the throat area, noting the color and odor
4. Resident response and participation in procedure
5. Signature and title of nursing staff member

SPUTUM SPECIMEN

OBJECTIVE

1. To identify, diagnose, and treat respiratory illnesses

LEVEL OF RESPONSIBILITY

Registered nurse, licensed practical nurse

EQUIPMENT

1. Sterile specimen container
2. Nonsterile gloves

PROCEDURE	RATIONALE
1. *Explain* procedure and purpose to the resident.	

PROCEDURE	RATIONALE
2. Assemble equipment and bring to resident's room.	
3. Wash your hands.	Hand washing prevents the spread of infection.
4. Put on gloves.	Use of gloves protects both the resident and the nurse and prevents the spread of infection.
5. *Instruct* resident to take a deep breath and then to force a cough and expectorate into the sterile container. A teaspoon full of sputum is all that is usually necessary for analysis.	This provides specimen from deep in lungs rather than sputum mixed with saliva collected in back of the throat.
6. Cover and label specimen immediately.	
7. Dispose of gloves properly.	
8. Wash your hands.	Hand washing prevents the spread of infection.
9. Prepare laboratory requisition form according to agency or facility policy.	
10. Store specimen according to laboratory requirements until transport to the laboratory is accomplished.	

DOCUMENTATION

1. Date and time specimen was obtained
2. Appearance of the specimen, noting any blood or appearance of color, such as green or yellow tinged
3. Resident response and participation in procedure
4. Signature and title of nursing staff member

WOUND SPECIMEN

OBJECTIVE

1. To identify, diagnose, and treat the early signs of wound infection

LEVEL OF RESPONSIBILITY

Registered nurse, licensed practical nurse

EQUIPMENT

1. Commercially prepared culture tube kit
2. Nonsterile gloves
3. Antiseptic skin cleanser

PROCEDURE	RATIONALE
1. *Explain* procedure and purpose to the resident.	
2. Assemble equipment and bring to resident's room.	
3. Wash your hands.	Hand washing prevents the spread of infection.
4. Put on gloves.	Use of gloves protects both the resident and the nurse and prevents the spread of infection.
5. Clean the area around the wound with the antiseptic cleanser.	This prevents the contamination of the wound specimen by bacteria from surrounding skin.
6. Gently roll the swab through any drainage from the wound. If there is no drainage, roll swab across wound area.	
7. Immediately place swab into culture tube. Follow directions enclosed for crushing ampule and storage of the tube until it can be transported to the laboratory for analysis.	
8. Dispose of gloves properly.	
9. Wash your hands.	Hand washing prevents the spread of infection.
10. Prepare laboratory requisition form according to agency or facility policy.	

DOCUMENTATION

1. Date and time specimen was obtained
2. Appearance of the wound and surrounding tissue
3. Appearance of redness, drainage, or heat at the wound site and surrounding area, noting the color and odor of any drainage
4. Resident's response to the procedure
5. Signature and title of nursing staff member

STOOL SPECIMEN

OBJECTIVES

1. To determine the presence of bleeding in the gastrointestinal tract, stomach, or small intestines
2. To determine the presence of bacteria, viruses, fungi, or parasites in the intestinal tract
3. To aid in medical diagnosis or to determine effectiveness of a specific therapy

LEVEL OF RESPONSIBILITY

Registered nurse, licensed practical nurse

EQUIPMENT

1. Bedpan or commode
2. Tongue depressor or sterile swab
3. Specimen container
4. Commercially prepared solution such as Hemoccult or guaiac (test for occult blood)
5. Nonsterile gloves

PROCEDURE	RATIONALE
1. *Encourage* the resident to *choose* the time for specimen collection according to the individual's regular elimination routine unless contraindicated by type of test to be performed or physician order.	If the specimen is to be tested for ova and parasites, it must be collected and taken to the laboratory immediately for examination while the stool is still warm. This maintains the parasites in viable condition. Other stool specimens are kept at room temperature until transport to the laboratory.
2. Wash your hands.	Hand washing prevents the spread of infection.
3. Provide for privacy.	
4. *Ask* resident to defecate into a clean, dry bedpan or commode. Immediately after defecation, remove approximately $2\frac{1}{2}$ centimeters of stool specimen using a tongue blade.	
5. Place specimen in specimen container and cover.	
6. If testing for occult blood, *teach* resident to use tongue blade to place a thin layer of stool in commercially prepared filter paper. Add hemoccult or guaiac solution to other side of paper. *Review* with resident the directions for reading results and repeating test if needed.	
7. Dispose of gloves properly.	
8. Wash your hands.	Hand washing prevents the spread of infection.
9. Prepare laboratory requisition form according to agency or facility policy.	

DOCUMENTATION

1. Date and time specimen was collected
2. Color, consistency, shape, odor, and amount of any unusual matter seen in the stool
3. Resident's understanding of the purpose and reaction to the collection process
4. Date and time specimen was sent to the laboratory for analysis
5. Signature and title of nursing staff member

URINE SPECIMEN

OBJECTIVES

1. To determine the presence of substances excreted by the kidneys
2. To assist in the diagnosis of pathological conditions

LEVEL OF RESPONSIBILITY

Registered nurse, licensed practical nurse

EQUIPMENT

1. Large gallon-size disposable container if a twenty-four-hour urine test is ordered
2. Small, sterile specimen container
3. Nonsterile gloves
4. Alcohol wipe
5. Ten milliliter syringe with needle

PROCEDURE	RATIONALE
1. *Explain* the procedure and purpose to the resident.	
2. Bring necessary equipment to the resident's room.	
3. Follow appropriate steps below for twenty-four-hour collection or Foley catheter collection.	

Twenty-Four-Hour Urine Collection

PROCEDURE	RATIONALE
1. If a twenty-four-hour urine collection is ordered, *instruct* the resident as completely as possible as to the reasons for the collection and how the collection process must be performed.	Thorough understanding promotes independence and self esteem for the resident and encourages compliance with the process.
2. *Encourage* the resident to set the time the collection will begin in the morning. The first morning voiding is always discarded.	The first voiding is concentrated because the length of time since last voiding is usually longer than between daytime voids, thus altering the results.
3. At the same time the next morning, the resident should void again. Place this specimen in the container as the last one to complete the twenty-four-hour collection.	
4. *Stress the importance* of placing all urine after the first urine of the day into the container.	Leaving any specimens out may alter the results of laboratory testing and result in the process being restarted the next day.

PROCEDURE	RATIONALE
5. Prepare laboratory requisition form according to agency or facility policy.	
6. Refrigerate specimen after proper labeling until it can be transported to the laboratory.	

Urine from a Foley Catheter

PROCEDURE	RATIONALE
1. Wash your hands.	Hand washing prevents the spread of infection.
2. Put on gloves.	Use of gloves protects both the resident and the nurse and prevents the spread of infection.
3. If collecting urine from a Foley catheter, cleanse port near bifurcation on catheter with alcohol wipe.	
4. Insert sterile needle with syringe.	
5. Aspirate approximately 9 to 10 cubic centimeters of urine.	
6. Place needle carefully into sterile specimen container and expel contents into container. Do not touch sides of container with the needle. Cover immediately.	
7. Dispose of gloves properly.	
8. Wash your hands.	Hand washing prevents the spread of infection.
9. Prepare laboratory requisition form according to agency or facility policy.	
10. Refrigerate specimen after proper labeling until it can be transported to the laboratory.	

DOCUMENTATION

1. Date and time specimen was obtained
2. Color, clarity, odor, and amount of specimen and any unusual findings, such as blood or mucous
3. Resident's response to specimen collection and understanding of the procedure and purpose
4. Signature and title of nursing staff member

GLUCOSE TESTING

OBJECTIVES

1. To determine blood glucose levels
2. To assess the level of control achieved by the resident's medication and/or diet

3. To assist the resident to attain a better understanding of testing methods and how to control blood glucose levels

LEVEL OF RESPONSIBILITY

Registered nurse, licensed practical nurse

EQUIPMENT

1. Glucometer calibrated to the currently used container of test strips
2. Cotton ball or clean (4 by 4 inch) gauze pad
3. Lancet (sterile)
4. Alcohol wipe
5. Bandaid
6. Nonsterile gloves

PROCEDURE	RATIONALE
1. If compatible with physician's orders, *encourage* resident to *choose* the time for glucose monitoring.	The ability to choose promotes independence for the resident.
2. At agreed upon time, *explain* the procedure and purpose to the resident. Careful *demonstration* and *explanation* of each of the steps over several days may be necessary before the resident can be expected to perform the task independently.	Blood glucose monitoring using the various steps associated with the glucometer can seem overwhelming initially.
3. Set glucometer according to the instructions in the glucometer kit.	Each manufacturer may have slightly different instructions or steps to follow.
4. Wash your hands.	Hand washing prevents the spread of infection.
5. Put on gloves.	Use of gloves protects both the resident and the nurse and prevents the spread of infection.
6. With alcohol wipe, cleanse side of fingertip to be used.	
7. Prick side of fingertip with sterile lancet. Hold finger in a downward position until a drop of blood is formed. Do not "milk" fingertip.	Milking may cause lysis of blood cells, thus giving an incorrect reading.
8. Touch blood to pad on test strip. Set timer on glucometer to specific instructions given with device.	
9. When timing is complete, wipe excess blood from test strip and place in slot in	

PROCEDURE	RATIONALE
glucometer. Set timer again as specified in instructions.	
10. It is possible to ascertain a general reading if a glucometer is not available by timing each step with a watch and second hand and then comparing color results with color coding on test strip bottle. This, however, can only be considered an estimation of the actual reading, since lighting, vision of the test performer, and possible color changes on the bottle itself may skew results.	
11. *Review, discuss,* and *instruct* the resident on a diet plan if an American Diabetes Association (ADA) meal plan and exchange list has been recommended by the physician.	Family and resident should be aware that an ADA diet is not complicated and is, in fact, a healthy diet for all family members.
12. *Instruct* the resident and family members on the pathophysiology and possible complications associated with diabetes.	Diabetes is a serious medical condition affecting many body systems, most prominently, the circulatory and cardiovascular system.
13. *Instruct* the resident and family on insulin administration, action, and storage.	
14. *Review* the resident's other prescribed and over the counter medications for possible drug interactions.	Some medications, such as diuretics and steroids, may affect the action of insulin.

DOCUMENTATION

1. Date and time specimen was obtained
2. Type of glucometer used and the results obtained
3. Details of teaching that was performed
4. Resident and family members' understanding of testing method, diet, drug interactions, administration, and storage of insulin
5. Return demonstration of glucose testing indicating degree of resident understanding and competence
6. Signature and title of nursing staff member

EVALUATION

1. The appropriate specimen will be obtained, stored, and analyzed in a professional manner to facilitate the treatment of the individual.
2. The resident will understand the purpose for each procedure.
3. The resident will assist with the procedure as necessary and appropriate to the specimen being collected.

OTHER SPECIMENS

There are several other specimen collection sites and techniques, such as cervical specimens, anal/rectal specimens, nasopharyngeal specimens, and blood specimens by venous puncture. These specimens are not commonly obtained by nursing staff or the resident but instead by other professionals and are, therefore, not discussed in this book.

	Wholly Compensatory
	Partly Compensatory
✔	Supportive-Educative

ANTIEMBOLYTIC STOCKINGS

OBJECTIVES

1. To help prevent thrombophlebitis
2. To provide support for persons with varicose veins or impaired circulation
3. To promote venous blood return and prevent pooling of blood in persons with temporarily restricted activity
4. To encourage resident's active involvement in completion of treatments

LEVEL OF RESPONSIBILITY

Registered nurse, licensed practical nurse, certified nursing assistant

POLICY

Elastic stockings should be removed and reapplied at least twice daily. Once each day the legs should be cleansed and the skin assessed.

EQUIPMENT

1. Elastic support stockings in correct size
2. Talcum powder
3. Basin with warm water
4. Soap, washcloth, and towel

PROCEDURE	RATIONALE
1. *Encourage* the resident to *choose* the time for applying and removing elastic stockings. The first time should be before getting out of bed each morning.	The ability to choose promotes independence for the resident.
2. At agreed upon time, *explain* procedure and purpose to the resident.	
3. Gather equipment and bring to the resident's room.	
4. Screen for privacy.	

PROCEDURE	**RATIONALE**
5. Wash your hands.	Hand washing prevents the spread of infection.
6. *Assist* resident to assume a Fowler's position (see Appendix B).	
7. *Encourage* resident to do as much for self as possible. This could be any or all portions of the activity, from applying talcum power to the entire application of the stockings.	Self performance of stocking application promotes independence and encourages exercise and range of motion.
8. Dust the ankles with talcum powder.	Dusting helps reduce friction and allows for easier application of the stocking.
9. Apply stockings by placing hands inside the stocking and gathering the material together down to the foot section. Pull the material outward while applying the stocking over the toes and working up to the ankle. At this point, check to be sure stocking is smooth and wrinkle-free. Pull toe section of stocking gently away from end of the toes.	Wrinkles can impede circulation and cause pressure ulcers. If stockings are tight around the tip of the toes, they may become constricted and circulation may be reduced.
10. Pull remaining portion of stocking up the leg by using the inside of the fingers and hands.	
11. When stocking is completely on the leg, check once again for wrinkles. If any are found, pull stocking down to the point of the wrinkle using the same method used to apply the stocking and adjust.	
12. *Instruct* the resident not to roll the stockings partially down.	Rolling will cause constriction of the venous circulation.
13. *Instruct* the resident and family members involved in the resident's care regarding methods of application and removal of the stockings.	
14. *Instruct* resident to report any discomfort, tingling, or loss of sensation at the stocking site to the nursing staff.	
15. *Encourage* resident to wash stockings with gentle soap, rinse well, and allow them to drip dry only.	Heat drying may weaken the elastic.
16. Wash your hands.	Hand washing prevents the spread of infection.

DOCUMENTATION

1. Date and time of stocking applications and removals
2. Condition of the skin before and after stocking applications
3. Any care given to the skin, such as application of lotion
4. Resident's tolerance of stockings
5. Resident's understanding of the reasons for the stockings
6. Resident's level of assistance with the activity
7. Signature and title of nursing staff member

EVALUATION

1. Resident will understand the purpose and necessity for wearing antiembolytic stockings.
2. The skin under the stockings will remain free of irritation.
3. Resident will participate in the application and removal of the stockings.
4. Resident will be able to report any signs of circulatory impairment.

ASSESSMENT OF TEMPERATURE—ORAL AND AXILLARY

OBJECTIVES

1. To obtain accurate measurement of body temperature
2. To encourage resident's involvement in and understanding of health assessment skills

LEVEL OF RESPONSIBILITY

Registered nurse, licensed practical nurse

EQUIPMENT

1. Thermometer
2. Watch

PROCEDURE	RATIONALE
1. Wash your hands.	Hand washing prevents the spread of infection.
2. *Teach* the resident the following key concepts of temperature assessment:	Education regarding procedures promotes independence for the resident through increasing knowledge and acquisition of a new skill.
a. Reason for temperature assessment.	Temperature can reflect the presence of an illness process. Classic illness symptoms are often not found in older people. Therefore, in older people an elevated temperature or a subnormal temperature can be very significant.
b. Appropriate timing for temperature assessment.	Inaccurate temperature readings will occur if an oral temperature is assessed immediately after drinking hot or cold fluids or if the resident has been smoking.
c. Frequency with which temperature should be assessed.	Physician may suggest the frequency of temperature assessment in order to elicit information regarding the resident's condition.
d. Choice of oral or axillary method.	Oral temperature is the easiest to perform on oneself, and is most commonly used. Axillary temperatures should be used if resident cannot close mouth around the thermometer or is unable to keep thermometer under the tongue.

PROCEDURE	RATIONALE
3. Use the following steps for procedure of temperature assessment, choosing the appropriate steps for oral or axillary temperature. If teaching this skill to the resident, *demonstrate* the procedure and *encourage* the resident to practice with you. Repeat teaching sessions until both you and the resident feel confident about the resident's ability to perform this new skill.	New skill acquisition often requires frequent teaching sessions with return demonstrations. Positive reinforcement will encourage the resident to continue to practice the new skill.

Oral Temperature Assessment

PROCEDURE	RATIONALE
1. *Encourage* resident to assume a sitting or lying position.	
2. If conventional thermometer is used, *encourage* resident to use her/his own clean thermometer. Shake thermometer down below level of scale.	Use of the resident's own thermometer prevents the spread of infection to other residents.
3. Place thermometer in mouth, well under tongue. Carefully close mouth around thermometer.	The most accurate reading will be obtained if thermometer is held under the tongue.
4. Keep thermometer in place for at least three minutes.	
5. Remove thermometer from mouth. Rotate thermometer so that temperature reading can be visualized. *Encourage* reading of the thermometer in a good light source.	Visualization of the reading may be difficult for an older person due to the smallness of the numbers and the color of the thermometer.
6. Shake thermometer down below scale level. Wash thermometer with cool water and soap. Return thermometer to its individual case.	
7. Wash your hands.	Hand washing prevents the spread of infection.

Axillary Temperature Assessment

PROCEDURE	RATIONALE
1. *Encourage* resident to assume a sitting or lying position. Loosen or remove clothing so that there is skin to skin contact in the axillary area.	For an accurate reading, the thermometer needs direct contact with skin.
2. If conventional thermometer is used, *encourage* the resident to use her/his own clean thermometer. Shake thermometer down below level of scale.	Use of the resident's own thermometer prevents the spread of infection to other residents.

PROCEDURE	RATIONALE
3. Place thermometer deep into axillary region. Resident then presses arm against thorax to keep thermometer in place.	
4. Hold thermometer in this position for at least five minutes.	
5. Remove thermometer from its position. Rotate thermometer so that reading can be visualized. *Encourage* reading of thermometer in good light source.	Visualization of the reading may be difficult for an older person due to the smallness of the numbers and the color of the thermometer.
6. For accurate assessment, add one degree to the number obtained on the thermometer.	Axillary temperatures are one degree lower than oral temperatures; therefore, axillary temperature plus one degree is a more accurate reflection of the resident's temperature.
7. Shake thermometer down below scale level. Wash thermometer with cool water and soap. Return thermometer to its individual case.	
8. Wash your hands.	Hand washing prevents the spread of infection.

DOCUMENTATION

1. Date and time of temperature assessment
2. Temperature reading, specifying whether oral or axillary temperature
3. Resident's ability and skill level to perform temperature assessment
4. Signature and title of nursing staff member

EVALUATION

1. The resident will be able to accurately measure her/his own body temperature.
2. The resident will express interest in learning about her/his own body temperature.

Glossary of Terms

Activities of Daily Living (ADL). Basic activities that one needs to perform in order to care for oneself. ADL include bathing, dressing, grooming, toileting, ambulating, and eating.

Clean Technique. Nonsterile method used to reduce rather than eliminate the number of micro-organisms during a procedure. It is used for activities not requiring a sterile environment, such as dressings to protect a wound, medication administration, ear drop application, and nose drop application.

Functioning. A person's ability to complete ADL and IADL.

Instrumental Activities of Daily Living (IADL). Basic activities that one needs to perform to care for oneself and one's surroundings. IADL include medication administration, shopping, meal preparation, housework, money management, telephone use, laundry, and transportation.

Nursing Staff. Refers to all members of the nursing team qualified to provide or supervise the activity being described. These members include registered nurses, licensed practical nurses, and certified nursing assistants.

Partly Compensatory Nursing System. The nursing system in which both the nurse and client have active roles in completion of self-care requirements.

Range of Motion (ROM). Refers to maintenance of mobility for all muscles and joints. The degree of mobility is individually determined by health status of the older adult.

Self Care. Defined by Orem as the "practice of activities that individuals initiate and perform on their own behalf in maintaining life, health and well-being." (George, 1990, p. 92)

Sterile Technique. Method of care designed to prevent and/or eliminate the introduction or spread of micro-organisms. It is used for catheterization, IV or IM medications, eye drops, surgical dressings, and to protect an individual who may have a compromised immune system.

Supportive-Educative Nursing System. The nursing system in which education and encouragement is provided by the nurse to the client while the individual performs self care.

Universal Precautions. Recommendations by the Centers for Disease Control (CDC) for prevention of contact with body fluids when giving resident care. Recommendations include using gloves; hand washing after each patient contact; using masks, protective eye wear, and gown if contact with bodily fluids is a possibility; and preventing injuries caused by needles or scalpel blades by never recapping needles or breaking needles before disposal in one-way disposable containers.

Wholly Compensatory Nursing System. The nursing system in which the nurse compensates for the client's inability to perform self care by actually doing the care for the individual.

REFERENCE

George, J. (Ed.). (1990). *Nursing theories: The base for professional nursing practice* (3rd ed.). Norwalk, CT: Appleton & Lange.

Glossary of Body Positions

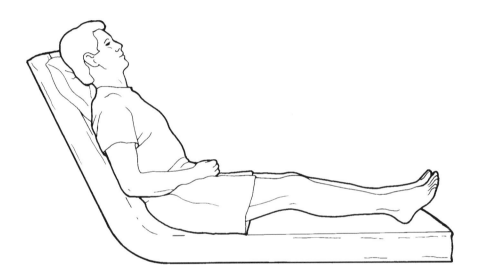

Fowler's Position

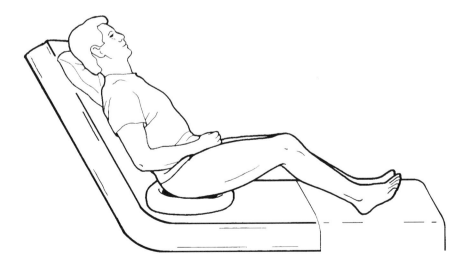

Semi-Fowler's Position on Bedpan

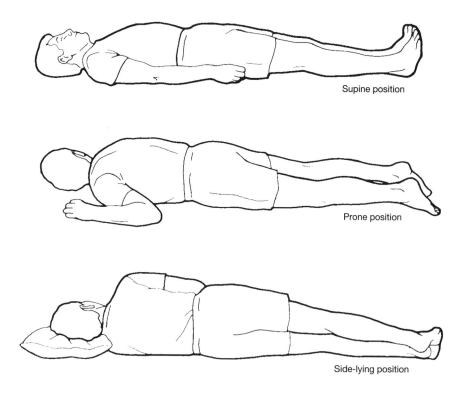

Supine position

Prone position

Side-lying position

Supine, Prone, and Side-lying Positions

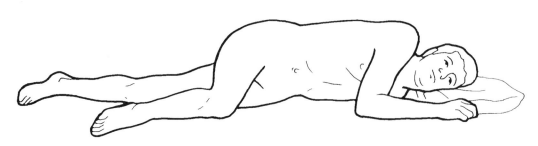

Position for Enema

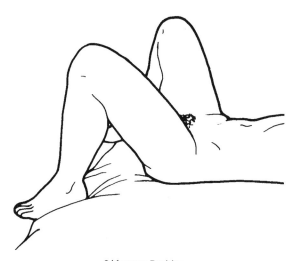

Lithotomy Position

appendix *C*

Bibliography

American Podiatric Medical Association, National Retired Teachers Association, American Association of Retired Persons. *Let's talk about foot care and you: A booklet for older adults.* Bethesda, MD: American Podiatric Medical Association.

Bernal, H. (1988). In-home medication checks with diabetics. *Home Healthcare Nurse, 6*(5), 14–18.

Brunner, L.S., & Suddarth, D.S. (1988). *Textbook of medical-surgical nursing* (6th ed.). Philadelphia: J.B. Lippincott Co.

Carlson, C., Griggs, W., & King, R. (Eds.). (1990). *Rehabilitation nursing procedures manual.* Rockville, MD: Aspen Publishers, Inc.

Centers for Disease Control. (1987). Recommendations for prevention of HIV transmission in health care settings. *Morbidity and Mortality Weekly Report, 36*(Suppl. 2–S).

Chinn, P. (Ed.). (1983). *Advances in nursing theory development.* Rockville, MD: Aspen Publishers, Inc.

Fitzgerald Miller, J. (1992). *Coping with chronic illness overcoming powerlessness* (2nd ed.). Philadelphia: F.A. Davis Co.

Gale, B. (1989). Advocacy for elderly autonomy: A challenge for community health nurses. *Journal of Community Health Nursing, 6*(4), 191–197.

Galias, D. (1989). *Resident care policies and procedures for nursing facilities.* Des Moines, IA: Briggs.

Gambert, S.R. (Ed.), Cooppan, R., & Gupta, K.L. (1990). *Diabetes mellitus in the elderly.* New York: Raven Press.

McCann Flynn, J., & Hackel, R. (Eds.). (1990). *Technological foundations in nursing.* Norwalk, CT: Appleton & Lange.

Oermann, M. (1991). *Professional nursing practice: A conceptual approach.* Philadelphia: J.B. Lippincott Co.

Orem, D. (1985). *Nursing concepts of practice* (3rd ed.). New York: McGraw-Hill Book Co.

Palmer, M. (1985). *Urinary incontinence.* Thorofare, NJ: Slack, Inc.

Pugliese, G. (Ed.). (1991). *Universal precautions: Policies, procedures and resources.* Chicago: American Hospital Publications.

Riehl-Sisca, J. (1989). *Conceptual models for nursing practice* (3rd ed.). Norwalk, CT: Appleton & Lange.

Sorenson, K., & Luckman, J. (1979). *Basic nursing: A psychophysiologic approach.* Philadelphia: W.B. Saunders.

Steffl, B. (Ed.). (1984). *Handbook of gerontological nursing.* New York: Van Nostrand Reinhold Co.

Suddarth, D.S., Bare, B.G., Batcheller, J.A.J., Bayley, E.W., Berkebilo, C.E., Bray, S.A., Dahlstrom, M.F., Finley, J.P., Goodman, D.B.P., Hoffman, L.A., Hravnak, M., Jacobs-Irvine, K., Kessler, C.A., Liddel, D.B., Marden, S.F., Temples-Mill, B., Morse, M.E., Pavel, J.N., Spittle, L., Witt, E.L., Weitkamp, T., Lavoie, D.J.B., Donaher, B.M., Farley, J.A., Selekman, J., Linthicum, D., Steinmuller, C., & Wilson, C.J. (1991). *The Lippincott manual of nursing practice* (5th ed.). Philadelphia: J.B. Lippincott Co.

Thomas, C. (Ed.). (1985). *Taber's cyclopedic medical dictionary.* (15th ed.). Philadelphia: F.A. Davis.

Wagnild, G., Rodriguez, W., & Pritchett, G. (1987). Orem's self-care theory: A tool for education and practice. *Journal of Nursing Education, 26*(8), 342–343.

Weinrich, S., & Boyd, M. (1992). Education in the elderly: Adapting and evaluating teaching tools. *Journal of Gerontological Nursing, 18*(1), 15–20.

Weinrich, S., Boyd, M., & Nussbaum, J. (1989). Continuing education: Adapting strategies to teach the elderly. *Journal of Gerontological Nursing, 15*(11), 17–21.

Wilson, A. (1988). Measurable patient outcomes: Putting theory into practice. *Home Healthcare Nurse, 6*(6), 15–18.

Wooldridge, P., Schmitt, M., Skipper, J., & Leonard, R. (1983). *Behavioral science and nursing theory.* St. Louis: C.V. Mosby Co.

Index

About the Authors

Laura A. Luc received her MSN in gerontological nursing from the University of Pennsylvania in 1983. Since that time she has worked as a clinical nurse specialist in acute care, long-term care, and community environments across the country. Presently, Ms. Luc is employed by Rush-Presbyterian-St. Luke's Medical Center and has developed an ongoing strategy to promote and design wellness programs with residents of a retirement community in suburban Chicago. Ms. Luc is a long distance runner and is currently pursuing a degree in exercise physiology with emphasis on exercise and older people.

Michele Beattie received her BSN from St. Xavier College in Chicago. She has worked extensively with older adults in various settings and positions as a home health nurse, home health supervisor, clinical manager, director of a home health/community service agency, and consultant to long-term care facilities. Currently, she is employed by Rush-Presbyterian-St. Luke's Medical Center in the position of geriatric assessment/admission coordinator.

DATE DUE

DEC 3 1	
APR 1 7 1995	
NOV 0 9 1995	
	Peel Off Pressure Sensitive
Library Store	